Life's Last Edit

Rahul Makwana

To Aarav, my son,

And to everyone else who is ready to take control and edit their life, this book is for you too.

Life can be messy, unpredictable, and at times overwhelming, but remember-change is just one decision away.

You have the power to take action, to rewrite your story, and to make each day a little better.

It all starts with the choice to begin.

Contents

Preface

Like many of you, I've tried countless methods for self-improvement. I've read book after book, watched motivational speeches, and listened to experts.

But even with all that knowledge, I still found myself stuck at times, unsure of how to apply it all in my everyday life.

Life's Last Edit is not another collection of abstract ideas or recycled advice. Instead, it's a guide that takes you through the lessons I've learned in my own journey.

These aren't theories or strategies I found in textbooks; they are lessons I've lived. I want to share with you the insights that have helped me find more clarity, purpose, and peace.

The truth is, there's no "one-size-fits-all" approach to life. But there are universal truths and tools that, when used intentionally, can help you take control of your journey.

This book is designed to be a toolkit-a collection of thoughts, ideas, and exercises to help you reclaim your narrative and start writing the life you truly want to live.

Introduction

Let me guess what you might be thinking:

"Rahul, there are already so many self-help books out there. Why should I pick up yours?"

That is a fair question.

And let me be honest—I am not here to convince you to buy another self-help book (maybe you just bought one) but, If you have read dozens of books, watched countless motivational videos, or tried to change your habits, but you still feel stuck...

If your life feels like it is exactly where it was years ago, then maybe this book can offer something different.

This is not one of those "copy-paste" self-help books, filled with the same old advice. It has its own unique insights, and I think you will notice that once you start reading.

Take this book as a bible of self-help books, I know it is a bold claim but as you read this book, you will know why I used these words. I'm not promising that this book will change your life.

The real change will come if you actively apply what you learn here. Otherwise, like many, you might find yourself reaching for the next self-help book.

In this case, please buy my books.
Just Visit, shop.bookiestalk.com.

"The true essence of life's last edit is about taking control of your narrative, trusting your journey, and recognizing that every experience, good or bad, contributes to the story you're writing—one small edit at a time."

Chapter 1

Life's True Compass

"Purpose is the quiet voice that guides us,
even when the path seems uncertain."

As Viktor Frankl says

"Ultimately, man should not ask what the meaning of his life is, but rather must recognize that it is he who is asked."

Think of it this way:

Instead of asking what life means to us, we need to realize that life itself is asking us a question. Each choice we make, each action we take, and the way we navigate suffering, love, and joy are all responses to life's questions.

Imagine you are someone struggling with your weight.

You have Two choices:

- Follow the right diet and exercise daily, or
- You can choose to stay the same.

Now, tell me, what would you choose? If I were in your place, I'd definitely fix my health first.

Start by deciding the kind of person you want to become, instead of getting stuck on *"Why am I here?"* If you're unhealthy, prioritize fixing your health first—because without good health, you might not live long enough to discover your purpose in life.

Whatever you do, from now until the day you die, will become the purpose of your life. The choices you make today will define the direction your life takes.

So remember, Don't find a purpose in your life, create one. Instead of spending endless time searching for life's purpose, focus on what needs to be done right now.

To give you a simple answer.

"Meaning of life isn't something we just find or wait for. It comes from within us, and we create it by the choices we make, how we act, and how we view the world."

Purpose of Life?

- A teacher who feels happy guiding students toward their goals might see their purpose in helping them succeed.
- An artist or musician who loves creating and sharing their work may find purpose in expressing themselves and inspiring others.
- Someone who's always learning and trying to improve might believe their purpose is to grow as a person and become the best version of themselves.

Simply put, everyone has a purpose in their mind, it is just that they don't know how to define their purpose.

So, starting today, shift your focus.

Help people whenever you can. Work on the things you love the most. Spend time with those you care about deeply.

And remember—you do not have unlimited time.

Stop wasting time on questions like:

- What is my purpose?
- Who am I?
- Why am I here?
- Why are people the way they are?
- Who created the Earth?
- What happens after death?
- Where is God?
- Is God even real?

Instead, focus on what truly matters:

- Prioritize what is important.
- Do not repeat the same mistakes.
- Take care of your health.
- Exercise regularly.
- Help others.
- Learn to love yourself.
- Be happy with what you have.

In the end, your purpose is not something you find. It is something you create—every single day, with every single decision.

Final Edits

1. Rather than focusing on the purpose of life, focus on what matters the most.
2. Instead of asking what life means to us, we should recognize that life itself is asking us a question.
3. Lastly, remember you don't have unlimited time.

Ending this chapter with a few quotes.

"Happiness doesn't come from external things; it comes from within, from how we choose to live each day."

-Eddie Jaku.

"Each man is questioned by life, and he can only answer to life by answering for his own life; to life, he can only respond by being responsible."

-Viktor Frankl.

Chapter 2

Power of Movement

"The present moment is all you ever truly have.
Don't wait for tomorrow to make a change—
start today."

When I was nineteen, I lost my big brother. He was everything I looked up to—always excelling in school, always someone I admired.

And then, in a single moment, he was gone. I wished I could turn back time to stop it, to bring him back.

That was the second time I had felt such a deep loss. The first was when I lost my father at the age of ten. After that, my mother raised me, my brother, and my sister on her own.

What I'm trying to say is, when something like this happens, you do not sit there thinking, "Oh, just forget the past, focus on the now, and everything will be fine." It is not that simple.

This philosophy doesn't hold much weight when such things happen in our own lives

At the end of the day, we are all human. We act based on what we feel is important, and at times, emotions may take control. What truly matters is how we choose to channel them.

You can either choose to stay alone for years and blame yourself for not doing anything or accept the reality and do what is necessary.

I will not lie to you—it is hard. But that is life. One thing I learned from my experience is this: open yourself up to someone you trust. Let everything out. Cry as loud as you need to. Say what you need to say. Just let those emotions go.

When My brother died, I did not cry at all. I just sat there, in denial, thinking, This cannot be happening. I barely spoke to anyone for an entire week.

In such situations, it can be difficult to take action and focus on what truly matters. It's never easy when we lose our loved ones.

However, when it comes to our own lives, we have the power to control them.

Food for Thought

Let's say you had a business—a successful one. You worked hard, achieved great things, and felt on top of the world. But then, for some reason, it all fell apart.

Hero to zero.

Your mind might be filled with thoughts like,

"I tried everything. I put all my money into it, and it still failed. What if it happens again? I might as well just find a job and play it safe."

You're right, doing a job is secure. You will not lose money. But here is the thing—if you have an idea that you truly believe could change your life or the lives of others, then it is worth giving it another shot.

This time, though, do not repeat the mistakes you made before. Learn from them. Improve. Remember, just because something did not work out in the past does not mean it never will.

You can always start again, from the ground up, and build something better. Do not blame yourself for the decisions you made back then. Instead, take the lessons with you and grow.

For example, imagine you are preparing for a competitive exam. Only 1,000 people will get selected, but there are 100,000 applicants. If you spend every day obsessing over those odds, it will be impossible to focus.

Now, let's say you don't pass.

You might think, **"The test was too hard. I gave it my all, and it still wasn't enough."**

But here's the thing: if you truly gave your best, you can be proud knowing you did everything you could. And if you fail? It's not the end. You learn from it, make adjustments, and try again.

The key is to learn from the mistakes and improve rather than give up.

"Focus on what matters the most, there is no point in thinking about what has to come and what has happened. Just focus on now, and do what is necessary rather than blaming yourself, time, people, or decisions you made. Always remember, the true power lies in the movement"

Final Edits

- The past is behind you, and the future is yet to come—so why not focus on the present?
- Spend your energy on what you can control, not on what you can't.
- Learn from your mistakes, but don't repeat them.
- And always keep in mind: life isn't as hard as it seems; it's the way you approach it that makes it challenging.

Chapter 3

70,000 thoughts

"You are not your thoughts. You are the awareness observing them."

On average, a person has around 60,000 to 80,000 thoughts in a single day! That's roughly 2,500 to 3,300 thoughts per hour or about 40 to 55 thoughts per minute.

Now here's the catch: most of these thoughts aren't new. They're often the same ones, repeated again and again—worries, plans, memories, and so on.

So, if you ever feel like your mind is spinning out of control, try zooming out for a moment. This will give you a different perspective.

With that being said, let's now talk about thoughts.

As Isaac Asim Says
"Your assumptions are your windows on the world. Scrub them off every once in a while, or the light won't come in."

Every day, you'll have thousands of thoughts, but what truly matters is which ones you choose to focus on.

If you focus on negativity, your day will likely reflect that mood, no matter how much you want to feel happy.

Instead, try to focus on the positive side. Yes, it can be challenging to stay positive during tough times, but if you shift your attention to what you can control, everything will start to feel a lot easier.

Again, it won't happen quickly, but once you step back from the problem and look at the bigger picture, you'll see what needs to be done.

Training Your Mind

Your mind doesn't know what is right or wrong, you're the one who decides it with the experience you had from the day you were born.

For example, let's say your parents told you that God doesn't exist. Growing up with that belief, you might accept it as truth.

But later, you start to question it and realize there's no clear answer about God's existence—some people believe, others don't, and no one has definitive proof either way.

On the other hand, if your parents told you that God does exist and you grew up reading books supporting this idea, you'd likely believe in God without questioning it much.

Over time, you'd be less likely to think about other possibilities, because the idea of God has always seemed like a fact to you.

"So no matter what people say, always Question your Beliefs."

Sometimes, you may not find the perfect answer right away, but along the way, you'll gain a deeper understanding of every perspective before reaching your final conclusion.

Remember, your mind doesn't automatically know what's true or false; it decides it with the experience you had. In the end, the brain puts everything together and tries to make sense.

So, no matter what you're told, always question it. As you explore, you'll discover new ways of thinking and form your own conclusions.

What I'm trying to say is, don't believe everything you see, hear or feel.

Instant Reply

Imagine someone said something hurtful about your mother or father. In that moment, your emotions take over—anger floods your mind, and without thinking, you lash out and hit them.

But if you had stepped back for a moment, you might have realized that they were just words—hurtful, but still just words.

Taking a breath would have helped you see that reacting wasn't necessary and that there was a better way to handle the situation.

For example, if someone insulted you in a language you don't understand, like Chinese or Sanskrit, you'd probably just ask, *"What does that mean?"*

You wouldn't get upset or react because the words don't have any impact on you.

Words are just sounds, and they only have the power we give them. Whether they're hurtful or kind, you can choose how to respond.

Now, of course, there are times when some things cross a line.

For example, if someone physically threatens you, then it's natural to protect yourself. But when it's just words, sometimes the best response is to step back, stay calm, and not let them get under your skin.

To make it simple, words only carry as much weight as you allow them to. It's often better to let them go than to react. Staying calm can give you more control over how you feel and respond.

Final Edits

- Every day, you'll have thousands of thoughts. What truly matters is which ones you choose to focus on. If you focus on negativity, your day will likely reflect that mood, no matter how much you want to feel happy. Remember, it will be hard to face problems but once you stay straight, everything will be fine. Don't run away from it, face it with a straight face.

- Words are just sounds, and they only have the power we give them. Whether they're hurtful or kind, you can choose how to respond.

- Don't believe everything you think. Thoughts are just thoughts.

- There is no need to watch every new movie, or TV show, watch reels, or read comments on X/(Twitter). Find better use of your time because whatever you do now, will be your future. Lastly, remember, you don't have unlimited time.

Chapter 4

Confident vs. Smart Person

"Confidence is not 'they will like me.' Confidence is 'I'll be fine if they don't.'" — Christina Grimmie

MS Dhoni once said

"You need to have a calm head in tough situations. I'd rather have a confident player who believes in their abilities than just a talented one who lacks that belief."

Imagine two friends, Aditi and Raj, working at a busy restaurant. Both are skilled at their jobs, but they react very differently under pressure.

Aditi has been at the restaurant longer and knows all the tasks perfectly. However, whenever it gets extremely busy, she starts to panic, doubts herself, and becomes hesitant in making decisions.

She'll often look to her manager for guidance or second-guess herself, which sometimes slows things down.

Raj, on the other hand, is relatively new but has a calm and confident approach. Even though he doesn't know everything, he trusts his instincts, stays focused, and doesn't get flustered when things go wrong.

If he makes a mistake, he quickly learns from it and adjusts without overthinking.

In a high-pressure situation, like when there's a sudden rush of customers, Raj's confidence in his abilities helps him stay composed and handle the workload efficiently. Aditi, despite her experience, gets overwhelmed and struggles to keep up.

The skill is important but it's confidence and a calm mindset under pressure that often make the real difference in performance.

Raj's belief in himself allows him to handle challenges with ease, even if he's not the most experienced.

The same goes for someone about to go on stage. Even if they know exactly what they need to say, lack of confidence can make things go wrong. They might forget their words or get too nervous.

On the other hand, someone who doesn't know exactly what they're going to say but isn't afraid of speaking will be more relaxed. They'll find a way to get through it, using their confidence to figure things out as they go.

MS Dhoni always says, rather than stressing about winning or losing a match, he encourages focusing on each ball, each moment—making sure you're giving your best effort consistently.

In simple words, focus on the process and not on the results. Instead of choosing to be either smart or confident, why not be both?

Prepare for what truly matters in your life, and when the time comes, take action with certainty, letting go of any worry about the outcome.

Two Kinds of People

Carol S. Dweck once said.
"People with a growth mindset believe that their abilities can be developed through effort and learning, while those with a fixed mindset see their skills as unchangeable."

For example, If you fail a math test, a fixed mindset might make you think, *"I'm just bad at math."* But with a growth mindset, you'd think, *"I didn't do well, but I can get better if I study more."*

So remember, whenever you face a setback, remind yourself it's a chance to grow, not proof of a permanent limit.

Whether you think you can or think you can't, you're right." - Henry Ford

Story of a Confident and Smart Person

There were two friends, Ravi and Sam, who decided to join a cooking class. Neither of them had ever cooked before.

On their first day, they both tried to make an omelet. Ravi's omelet turned out great, but Sam was a mess. Sam felt embarrassed and thought, *"I'm just not good at cooking. I'll never get it right."*

From that point on, whenever they tried a new recipe, Sam would get frustrated quickly. He started avoiding more difficult dishes, thinking there was no point in trying.

Ravi, on the other hand, saw his cooking mistakes as a part of learning. When he messed up a recipe, he'd laugh it off, think about what went wrong, and say, *"I'll get it right next time."*

He asked the instructor for tips, practiced at home, and even watched videos to improve. For him, every mistake was just a step toward getting better.

After a few months, Ravi could cook a variety of dishes confidently, while Sam was still struggling and mostly stuck to making only simple dishes.

Ravi's growth mindset helped him see challenges as opportunities to learn, while Sam's fixed mindset held him back from improving because he believed he was naturally "bad" at cooking.

The difference between them was that Ravi believed in growing with practice, while Sam thought he couldn't get better, so he gave up too soon.

The growth mindset can open up new skills and possibilities, while a fixed mindset can keep you from reaching your potential.

At the end of the day, what you say to yourself and what you believe makes a huge difference in your decision-making.

Final Edits

- Rather than being a smart person, be a confident person. Prepare for what matters the most in your life, and when the right time comes, perform the task without worrying about what will happen next.
- The growth mindset can open up new skills and possibilities, while a fixed mindset can keep you from reaching your potential.
- You're what you think about every single day. Don't watch, hear, or feel everything around you. Decide what matters the most.

Remember, the right mindset will take you wherever you want to go. Be confident but don't forget to prepare otherwise, you will have a voice but it won't have meaning.

Chapter 5

Life's Little Seeds

"Success is the sum of small efforts, repeated day in and day out." — Robert Collier

Once we plant seeds in the soil, it takes some time to grow as a tree. You can't expect the result within a day or month.

You might use chemicals to speed up the process, but it will harm everyone who consumes products from that plant in the long run.

Similarly, when adding a new habit to your life, avoid taking shortcuts. If you do, there's a good chance you'll end up back where you started.

For example, one fine day you thought of adding a few habits and quitting a few.

Here is what you aim to quit:

- You want to quit drinking coffee.
- You want to quit consuming sugar.
- You want to quit smoking cigarettes.
- You want to quit eating packaged foods.

Here is what you want to add:

- You want to start exercising.
- You want to start reading books.
- You want to begin meditating.
- You want to start running.

Now, you can take the natural, steady approach—like nurturing a tree—or you can choose to force the process, much like a farmer experimenting with chemicals for quicker results.

Let's say, you decide to make all these changes at once. You quit everything you've always wanted to and added all the good habits at once.

At first, everything felt great. You had a surge of energy and motivation. You woke up early, worked out, ate healthy, meditated, and checked off everything on your to-do list.

It seemed like you were finally on the right path, and the progress felt exciting. But after about five days, things started to change.

The energy you once had began to fade, and the tasks that once felt empowering now felt like a burden.

You started feeling tired and overwhelmed, and the excitement slowly turned into resistance. The pressure of trying to maintain all those changes at once began to weigh on you, and you found yourself thinking,

"Maybe I bit off more than I could chew."

("If you want to explore more about the emotions and experiences you might face when quitting or adopting a new habit, visit the "Dopamine (Detox) chapter 8").

Now, it's like you're pushing yourself just to keep going.

Why does this happen?

This happens because our brain doesn't like when we make huge changes at once. This is not the same for everyone but most of the people are like that.

The reason we often resist change is because we fear the unknown—uncertainty, discomfort, and the idea of stepping out of our comfort zone.

Our brains are wired to protect us, so when we make sudden shifts in our routines, it perceives this as a threat. It's like an alarm going off, signaling us to return to what feels safe and familiar.

The brain doesn't care if a change is good or bad; it just wants to keep us safe in what feels familiar.

So, when we try to grow, the brain naturally resists and pulls us back to what feels familiar, even if it slows down our progress.

The good news is, if you stick with a new habit for a few more days, your brain will adjust, and the change will become easier and more natural.

Now, here is the big BUT.

If you force yourself to adopt more than 1 habit at once then it will be very hard for your brain to accept the change unless and until you're David Goggins.

As he says
**"The only person who was going to turn my life around was me.
The only way I could get turned around was to put myself
through the worst things possible that a human being could
ever endure."**

This does not mean you need to push your body to extreme
limits. Instead, it means gradually pushing yourself beyond your
comfort zone and embracing growth.

Initially, this process might feel like suffering, but over time,
you will look back and thank yourself for the effort. Growth,
much like a tree, takes time and patience.

Let it happen naturally, and the results will be long-lasting.

Grow Like a Tree

If you don't want to be like David Goggins (I get it, it's not that easy to be like him), so why not be like James Clear. Who says,

"Making a choice that is 1 percent better or 1 percent worse seems insignificant at the moment, but over the span of moments that make up a lifetime, these choices determine the difference between who you are and who you are. Success is the product of daily habits—not on could be-in-a-lifetime transformations"

For example, if you want to start reading books. So rather than forcing yourself to read for 60 minutes, why not read for either 5 or 10 minutes?

This may seem little at the start but after 30 or 60 days you will start to read for 30 to 60 minutes and you won't even notice this time jump.

Remember, after a few days, you will have thoughts like **"This is nothing, I can read for more than 10 minutes"**.

Just don't do such things.

Imagine you decide to read for 60 minutes instead of just 10. You stick to this for about three days, but on the fourth day, you might feel like skipping it.

You might think, *"60 minutes? I've already read for three days straight. So it's okay to skip a few days. Next time, I'll read for 120 minutes to make up for it."*

You might start thinking, *"All right, 120 minutes is like 12 days' worth of reading. So I'll skip the next 12 days, and then on the 13th day, I'll finish the entire book."*

(spoiler alert, you won't feel like reading after skipping 12 days. Don't try to fool yourself.)

Once that thought creeps in, there's a good chance you won't pick up the book anytime soon.

Maybe after a few months, you'll get back to reading for just 10 minutes a day. Then, you'll feel motivated again to push for 60 minutes, and the cycle starts all over again.

So why not just start with small and when you feel like it, add 10 minutes on top but if you don't follow this then, The day will come when you find yourself reading Instagram comments instead of a book.

Normally, it takes around 18 days to as long as 254 days to build new habits.

So stick with whatever habit you want to adopt otherwise, the chances are you will try your best to move away from the habit.

Many people find that committing to 30 days is a great start—just long enough to establish a foundation without overwhelming yourself.

30 days is like a warmup. At first, start small, and gradually increase the time when it feels right. Just don't make a huge jump,

While doing so, make sure you're Consistent and keep reading books for 5 to 10 minutes or more. After a month your brain will start to accept the new change.

The key to remember is, Don't skip a day, week, or month.

Now, if you're still finding it hard to move forward then let's talk about Matt D'Avella who Introduced us to the 2-days rule.

2-Day Rule

Introduced by Matt D'Avella. This is one of the best things you can apply in your life, if you're finding it hard to add new habits.

The idea behind this rule is that you can miss a day, but never miss two days in a row.

How the 2-Day Rule Works

Sometimes you'll miss a day of your new habit—whether it's exercising, reading, or working on a project. The rule doesn't punish you for missing a day, but it encourages you not to let it become a habit.

- **Stay Consistent:** The key is to never miss two days in a row. If you miss a day, get back on track the next day.
- **Keep Going:** By following this rule, you maintain a sense of commitment, even on days when you feel lazy or distracted. Don't think, *"I missed it."* Instead, think, *"It's okay, I missed a day. I'll get back on track tomorrow."*

The 2-Day Rule works because it allows for imperfection while still encouraging regular effort. It teaches you to bounce back quickly and keep going, preventing small setbacks from snowballing into larger problems.

Yes, it will be hard at first but once you keep going for months, things will get easy.

Just try it for a few days.

One of the best ways is to take plain paper and make 30 boxes. When you perform the habit, make a cross on the box and when you skip, leave the box empty.

Remember

"Great things take time. Keep going, even when you can't see the end yet."

Key For Everything

Consistency is key to everything, whether you want to build new habits or quit bad ones.

When you try to add new habits, there will be times you feel like skipping a few days. In those moments, remind yourself why you started in the first place.

And yes, despite your best efforts, you might still skip a few days—and that's okay. You don't have to be perfect; you just need to stay consistent.

Remember, only you can change yourself. No one will come and say, *'Hey, get up, it's time for you to live a healthy life.'*

I know there will be days when you don't feel like reading, but those are the moments to remind yourself, *'What are you doing? If you can scroll through social media for hours, surely you can read for just 5 minutes.'*

When you call yourself out, you become more aware of your actions—the good, the bad, and everything in between. The same principle applies to exercise, waking up early, or even working on new business ideas.

As Robin Sharma says **"Change is hard at first, messy in the middle, and gorgeous at the end."**

In the end, keep this in your mind forever

"Consistency isn't about perfection; it's about showing up regularly, even if the effort is small. Over time, this steady effort leads to real, meaningful changes that can reshape your habits, mindset, and life."

Don't Go After

As Mahendra Singh Dhoni says.

"Focusing too much on the outcome can lead to anxiety and mistakes while trusting the process allows people to stay grounded and perform at their best."

In short, don't focus on the result, focus on the process. This can be hard to follow but once you understand the power of process, things will get easy.

This is true right, if you think about results all the time then you won't have time to work on your goals. For example, if you want to start a new business and if you only think about,

- How much money will it make?
- how big business can become?
- what if a business fails?
- How will I be able to make money?

If you focus on these things then you will have a hard time doing work because you're worrying more about the future rather than focusing on what needs to be done.

Of course, there will be days when you will question yourself for the decisions you took but if you're confident about your business then the past decisions won't bother you much.

But if your business idea and planning is trash then yes, you should question everything.

"If the roots
are deep,
there is no
reason to fear
the wind"

One more thing.

When I was doing my research, I found out that most of the author says *"Replace a bad habit with a good ones"* This is true but there is a better way to do it, let's explore it.

For example,

Let's say Raj has developed a nightly habit of scrolling through social media before bed.

The thing is, Raj knows that his habits are affecting his sleep quality, leaving him tired and unfocused the next day.

At first, it didn't seem like a big deal—it was just one bad night of sleep here and there. But over time, it became a pattern.

He noticed that his energy levels were consistently low, and his ability to concentrate at work was slipping. For years, Raj brushed it off, telling himself it was just a temporary phase or something he could manage.

However, when his lack of sleep started impacting his health—like feeling more stressed, getting headaches, and not being able to focus on the things that mattered—he realized that the issue was far bigger than he had initially thought.

Then, he decided to replace his late-night scrolling with reading.

(The good news was that he became aware of his bad habit— something many people don't even realize is affecting their sleep. Most don't understand why they struggle to sleep properly or wake up feeling tired.)

At first, the new habit felt refreshing, and he began to notice some improvement in his sleep quality. But after a few days or weeks, old habits crept back in.

He found himself reaching for his phone again. Before long, he was back to scrolling at night, frustrated that the new habit didn't stick as he had hoped.

Why Replacements Won't Work All the Time

If scrolling was a way to de-stress, escape from feelings of loneliness, or simply disconnect from the demands of the day, then replacing it with reading doesn't directly address those needs.

So first, understand the triggers and once you do that, things will get very easy.

Trigger, a new word. Let's make it simple.

A trigger is something that sets off a thought, feeling, or reaction in you. It could be a sound, place, memory, or even a smell that makes you feel a certain way, often bringing up past emotions or habits.

Triggers are like buttons—when something presses them, it can influence how you feel or act, often without you even realizing it.

Now, Let's take my example, I used to drink tea and have snacks around 3 pm every single day. It had become such a routine that I didn't even think twice about it.

I wasn't the kind of person who ate out often, so I never saw it as a big deal. But the bad news was, I never truly realized how this seemingly harmless habit had slowly taken over my daily life.

My weight started to increase, and I didn't even realize it. At the time, I was around 75kg. I never went above 65kg in my 27-year life and here, I'm with a fat face and a big belly.

The bad news was, I was never hungry at 3 pm ever but as I started to think about tea and snacks, I couldn't stop.

I did try to replace the snacks with fruit or nuts but even that didn't work as I was always thinking about eating the snacks with tea.

Whenever I see tea, I think about eating snacks and when I see snacks, I think of drinking tea. So Tea and snacks were the triggers. I had been doing this for years without really noticing the impact it was having on me.

It became such a normal part of my routine that I didn't think twice about it. Then one day, my wife said, "You're eating out and having too much processed food."

Like most people, I didn't pay much attention to it. But one day, when I looked at myself in the mirror, the first word that came out of my mouth was, "Shit."

When I realized my triggers, I stopped going into the kitchen after 1 PM, Never brought snacks into my room, and whenever I felt like eating snacks, I always drank 1 glass of water.

It was like shifting my focus from tea and snacks to somewhere else.

And yes, it wasn't as easy as it sounds. It was tough. You don't realize how hard it was for me to give up something I had been eating every single day for a whole year.

What I realized from this was, don't just replace bad habits with good ones without understanding the root cause. If you don't address the underlying reasons, you'll find yourself right back where you started, just like Raj.

Final Edits

- Our brain resists big changes, avoiding drastic shifts. Start small, and build from there.
- Consistency is the key to progress. Focus on the process, not just the outcome.
- Identify your triggers and address them, rather than simply replacing bad habits with good ones without understanding the cause.
- And remember, it all ties back to the cue, routine, and reward."

without pain,
there is no gain.

Chapter 6

For Better Tomorrow

"Small daily improvements over time lead to stunning results." — Robin Sharma

Raj is a regular guy with a pretty typical day-to-day life. He's got a decent job, a small group of friends he hangs out with, and a list of things he always says he'll *"get around to"*—like learning to cook, saving for a trip, or reading more books.

But, lately, he's been feeling worn out. Each night, he tells himself, *"Tomorrow, I'll get organized."* But then tomorrow comes, and things don't go as planned.

Raj wakes up to the alarm he's snoozed twice already. He's running a little late, so he skips breakfast, grabs his phone, and scrolls through social media as he gets dressed.

At work, he ends up working through lunch, only stopping to check his phone for a few "quick" minutes (which turns into 20), and by the end of the day, he feels exhausted.

When he gets home, he has a vague plan to work out or maybe start reading that book he bought last month.

Instead, he crashes on the couch, and before he knows it, he's three episodes into a series. He goes to bed feeling like the day disappeared on him. And the next day, the same thing happens again.

Doesn't it sound like your story?

This was my story years ago but I changed it because of the same reasons. Like feeling busy all the time, doing everything and not finishing a single thing, saying I will change myself and yet, nothing happens.

Back to Raj's life.

After feeling like shit. Raj decides to change the way he is living. So he changed a few things.

- **Mornings**: Instead of jumping right into his phone, he starts with 5 minutes to plan out three things he wants to focus on. This simple list—like *"things he will do during the day"*
- **Work Blocks:** He starts using the Pomodoro Technique to avoid getting distracted. It's not perfect, but it helps him cut back on constant task-switching, and he actually finishes what he starts.
- **Evening Routine:** He replaces Netflix with a bit of reading before bed. He starts with just 10 minutes, and some nights, he's able to keep going; other nights, he just unwinds.

Earlier, he used to feel like moving from one thing to the next without a sense of purpose. Routine has helped him focus on what's important to him, and he's actually seeing progress now.

If you're still living your life as Raj was living then just like Raj, you need to change the way you're living.

You can also use the Techniques Raj tried:

1. The Eisenhower Matrix by Dwight D. Eisenhower.

- **What it is:** A method that helps you prioritize tasks based on importance and urgency.
- **How it works:** You split your tasks into four categories—urgent & important, important but not urgent, urgent but not important, and neither.
- **Example:** Prepping a big presentation is important but not urgent, so you can start it early rather than waiting for it to become urgent. Using a phone is not urgent or even important, so don't waste your time on it.

As Dwight D. Eisenhower says
"What's important usually isn't urgent, and what's urgent usually isn't important."

2. Pomodoro Technique by Francesco Cirillo.

* **What it is:** A focus method where you work for 25 minutes, then take a 5-minute break.
* **How it works:** You set a timer for 25 minutes and work on just one task, then take a quick break to reset. If you want, you can also work for 90 minutes and take a rest. Do this after sometime, don't rush it otherwise, you might get tired. Maybe, after a week, add 10 to 20 minutes on top of 25 minutes.

As Francesco Cirillo Says -
"If you do what you need to, you're surviving. If you do more than what you need to, you're thriving."

3. The Rule of 3 by Chris Bailey.

- What it is: A focus method where you work for 25 minutes, then take a 5-minute break.
- **How it works:** You set a timer for 25 minutes and work on just one task, then take a quick break to reset. If you want, you can also work for 90 minutes and take a rest. Do this after sometime, don't rush it otherwise, you might get tired. Maybe, after a week, add 10 to 20 minutes on top of 25 minutes.

As Chris Bailey Says-
"Busyness is no different from laziness when it doesn't lead you to accomplish anything."

Remember, these methods will only work if you stay consistent. Yes, it will take some time but eventually, you will get there.

Don't Force Yourself to Wake Up Early. It's not the hour you wake up that matters—it's what you do with your time.

Whether you start your day at 5 a.m. or 10 a.m., having a solid plan for how to use your time is what makes the difference.

Imagine, you're waking up at 4 am because you read somewhere that successful people wake up early but instead of working on important things, you start watching movies, scrolling on social media, or talking to someone on call.

So remember, everyone has different rhythms, schedules, and lifestyles. Just because early mornings work well for some people doesn't mean they're right for everyone.

Don't believe in the idea that working all night is bad and waking up early is a sign of success. Everyone has 24 hours, in the end, it depends on how each plans to use it.

Lastly, it will take some time to adopt a new routine. So don't get bored and go back to the previous one. If you want to know more about how to adopt new habits, *please visit Life's Little Seeds (chapter. 5)*.

"The early morning has gold in its mouth, but only if you're actually awake enough to appreciate it."

Final Edits

- Living without a routine is like living without direction. Without a routine, you'll find yourself wasting time on whatever comes your way.
- There is no need to wake up early, Don't believe in the idea that working all night is bad and waking up early is a sign of success. Play around and see what works best for you.
- Use Techniques that Raj used in his life to build routines.
- Always remember, nothing is impossible. You're the only one who is making it impossible.

Chapter 7

Writing A Thoughts

"Write what should not be forgotten." — Isabel Allende

As Mae West says
"Keep a journal, and someday it will keep you."

If you have never written a journal before, you might find this idea a bit strange. You may wonder, *"Why should I write down what I do or think? What purpose does it really serve?"*

I was that person years ago, too. But the day I started journaling, I realized its incredible power to free me from the constant cycle of overthinking.

It's simple, yet it helps you feel so much better. How? That's what you're about to discover.

How to Start Journaling

- **Set a Time:** Choose a time that fits into your day, such as the morning or night. For me, nighttime works perfectly. Because you've lived through the day, and by writing down your thoughts on paper, you release them, leaving your mind free and clear for a peaceful night's sleep.
- **Choose a Method:** Start with paper journals for a tactile feel or digital apps if you prefer typing. If you ask me, a notebook is perfect. This feels right rather than relying on apps. Try out both things and see what works best for you.
- **Pick a Format:** Decide between structured (like prompts) or unstructured journaling. You can find structured journals online which will have a few questions that you can fill up.

Or you can write like I do *"Write whatever you feel at the time you're writing it"*

Also, I feel, don't buy journals, just get a plain notebook and pen.

Don't waste your money on them, but if you have extra cash, buying one won't hurt. And while you're at it, visit **shop.bookiestalk.com**—you'll find journals there too.

Tips and Tricks for Journaling

- **Start Small:** Commit to just 5-10 minutes a day to build the habit. Don't try to write it for 30 to 60 minutes. Chances are you will get bored and you will never pick the pen again.

- **Use:** If you're finding it hard to what to write, use something like, *"What am I grateful for today?"* *"What did I learn today?"* *"Where did I spend most of my time"* *"What kind of activity did I do"* *"Are you happy with how your day went"*
- Or, just write whatever comes to mind. There is no structure on what and what not to write.

- **Don't Overthink:** Write freely without worrying about grammar or coherence. Look, no one is going to read your journal. So write whatever you want and however you want.

- **Set a Reminder:** Use reminders, so you don't forget to write a journal.

- **Reflect Monthly:** Review your journal every month to see your growth and revisit important thoughts. If you want, try to read your journal every Sunday. This will give you some idea on where you made mistakes and where you spend most of your time.

How to Make Journaling a Habit

Habits—we won't spend much time here. For a deep dive, check out Life's Little Seeds (Chapter 5). But if you want a quick, simple answer... here we go.

- **Consistency:** Commit to journaling daily or a few times a week, even if it's just a few sentences. Write whatever you can, even a few words are enough. Just write, don't skip it just because you don't feel like it or your day didn't go as you planned it.

- **Start Small:** If writing a full page seems daunting, start with a sentence or two.

- **Tie it to an Existing Habit:** Journal right after another daily habit, like having your morning coffee. Or before you go to bed, try to write a few things on paper. Or after dinner. Or after reading a book.

- **Reward Yourself:** Celebrate small wins (like a completed week) to reinforce the habit. After a week of journaling consistently, treat yourself by doing something you've been wanting to do but kept putting off. Like, eating something, going out, or watching a movie in the theater.

As Mina Murray says

"Journaling is like whispering to one's self and listening at the same time."

Story Time

If you're still not convinced to start journaling, this story will change your mind.

Remember the Raj, the same Raj who was struggling because of his bad routines. That same Raj had been Journaling for years and this is what it taught him.

It started out as a simple way to remember his days, but over time, his journal became something more.

This happened because he added journaling to his routine. It was his safe place, the one spot where he could be completely honest about his feelings.

Every good moment, every heartbreak, every small victory and big mistake—it was all there, page after page.

One day, Raj found himself in a tough spot. He felt that familiar, nagging fear he had dealt with in the past.

Little things seemed bigger than they should be, and his mind kept running in circles, filling up with worry. He was frustrated, feeling like he was back where he'd started.

One day as he was writing a journal, He flipped through the pages. He found an entry from a few years back that felt almost like it was written for him now.

"Today, I feel like I'm not enough, that the world's demands are too much for me. But I've been here before, and I made it through. I can let this be just a moment, not my entire reality."

Raj smiled. Reading those words, written by his younger self, made him realize that his worries hadn't been as big as they'd felt. He'd built them up in his head.

Another line caught his eye: **"Every struggle has a beginning, a middle, and an end. I am not my struggle; I am the person who walks through it."**

As he read this, Raj felt a kind of calm settle over him. He realized he was stronger than he'd given himself credit for. He had faced tough times before and came out on the other side, and this time would be no different.

With that reassurance, Raj went back to his day with a clearer mind.

He didn't try to force himself to feel better instantly; Instead, he took small steps, doing things he enjoyed—going for walks, making a simple meal, calling an old friend. Slowly, he felt more like himself again.

A few weeks later, he wrote a new entry:

"I felt lost, but looking back reminded me that I'm stronger than I thought. I've been through these ups and downs, and I always find my way. The next time I struggle, I'll remember that it's just another moment, and it will pass."

Chapter 8

Dopamine (Detox)

"True freedom is in choosing what we give our attention to, not being a slave to every impulse." — Cal Newport

Time to talk about one of the important parts of humans, Dopamine (we will also talk about Dopamine Detox too). This will be the longest chapter in the book and the only one you'll need to truly understand how dopamine and dopamine detox work.

So let's Begin.

I tried dopamine detox for 7 days from 10th July to 17th July 2023. Did it change my life, the answer is YES but how and in what sense is what we're going to talk about?

But before we get to the details, let's establish some essential ground rules.

- **Avoid Digital Entertainment:** Skip social media, gaming, and TV. Instead, read a book or go for a walk.
- **Limit Sugary & Processed Foods:** Choose healthier snacks like fruit or nuts instead of sugary treats.
- **No Unnecessary Purchases:** Resist impulse shopping; spend time journaling or with loved ones instead.
- **Replace Scrolling with Hobbies:** Engage in creative activities like drawing, cooking, or exercising instead of aimless scrolling.
- **Embrace Silence & Solitude:** Avoid background noise like music or podcasts during quiet moments. Focus on being present.

Yes, it will be hard but as someone says,

Do hard things, have an easy life; do easy things, have a hard life.

These are advanced rules, and you don't need to follow all of them at once. I went all-in because I was curious to see how my body and mind would react.

You can start small—maybe cut out social media or skip OTT apps for a few days. Even just one change can make a noticeable difference in how you feel physically and mentally.

Don't let the thought of quitting everything overwhelm you. Pick one rule, commit to it for a few days, and observe what happens.

No excuses—just give it a try.

Is it Time for a Dopamine Detox?

No one knows what is the right time for Dopamine Detox because, from your perspective, you're living a perfect life. You might be like, I'm doing good, why do I need to make any change?

To know whether you need Dopamine Detox, just answer these questions.

- Are you finding it challenging to stay focused on a single task?
- Do you often catch yourself mindlessly scrolling through social media or spending excessive time on your phone?
- Do you feel you're not having fun doing things that you used to enjoy the most?
- You're finding 30-minute videos or even movies too long and you're scrolling on Reals, TikTok, and YouTube Shorts for hours.
- You're having a hard time sleeping at night, hence you using a smartphone in your bed for hours?
- You don't like to do exercise because you feel you don't have time.

Answer these 6 questions with 100% honesty. No one is watching you, just answer to yourself.

Now even if the answer is YES for 2 to 3 questions then you need to try Dopamine Detox.

I get it—it's tough to give up habits you've been attached to for years. But if you genuinely want to improve yourself and build a better future, these changes won't feel impossible unless you let them be.

Assuming you want to try Dopamine Detox, it makes sense to understand what Dopamine and Dopamine Detox are.

Even if you're not planning to try it, take a moment to read and understand why you shouldn't give away your dopamine so easily to everything around you.

What is Dopamine and Dopamine Detox?

To make it simple, Dopamine is a neurotransmitter that is sort of a messenger that tells you when to feel good.

For example, when you drink coffee, your brain releases dopamine, making you feel energized and alert.

The issue with dopamine is that if you drink coffee every day for a year, your brain becomes less responsive.

Over time, the same cup of coffee won't give you that initial boost of energy—it's like your brain gets used to it.

Take masturbation as an example. If you do it every day for a year, the pleasure and satisfaction won't feel as intense over time.

On the other hand, if you space it out—say once a week or month—it tends to feel more enjoyable and fulfilling. This is because your brain has time to reset and respond more strongly.

Why do you feel this way?

When you start drinking more than one cup of coffee each day, your brain begins to adjust, making that extra caffeine the

'new normal.'

Over time, instead of feeling energized after just one cup, your brain will crave even more caffeine to feel the same boost you got when you first started drinking coffee.

This is why people become addicted to substances like alcohol or drugs. Over time, the brain starts to crave more and more to feel the same effects, and before they realize it, they may become dependent.

As someone said **"Moderation is the key to everything"**

This is where the Dopamine Detox comes in, Anyone can try Dopamine Detox, but it's essential for those who no longer feel joy or satisfaction from activities like drinking coffee, masturbating, or even having sex.

If these experiences have lost their spark, it's likely a sign that your brain's reward system is overstimulated and needs a reset.

The solution is not to release Dopamine too often.

Benefits of Dopamine Detox

The Dopamine Detox doesn't mean, you have to stop having SEX but it rather means, you have to cut down on unnecessary things. So you can focus more on the things that matter.

- More focus and clarity
- improved self-control
- Increased appreciation for simple things
- Reduced anxiety
- Better sleep quality

All these benefits or rules may sound basic but once you try out Dopamine Detox and experience it all, **you will realize how it feels to be a normal person who enjoys everything about life.**

Day 1

I'm someone who loves coffee and I'm someone who doesn't want to quit. This was the biggest challenge for me.

I usually wake up every day at 5:00 AM and do all the normal things, like, brush, take pop, and freshen up.

At around 5:30 minutes, normally I make coffee for myself and drink the same for about 30 minutes on the roof of my house. This is one of my favorite things to do in the morning.

I also walk for 30 minutes while I drink coffee, it feels amazing. I enjoy every second till I finish my coffee.

Now, if you love coffee as I do then you already know that it's not that easy to quit. Even if you manage to quit for a day, the day feels empty.

That's what happened on the first day which was 10th July 2023. Today, I woke up at 5:00 AM and did all the normal things.

The hard part started at 5:30 AM, I didn't know what to do. For about 10 minutes, I thought about drinking coffee but then I thought it's only 7 days, so let's go with it.

So what I did was, I started working on the article that I was supposed to write after 8:00 AM.

I wrote for about 2 hours and finished a few articles. I read the same and I realized *"Whatever I have written is trash."* No one will enjoy reading, even Search Engines won't like it.

So I deleted everything. Wasted 2 hours. The problem was, I really wanted to drink coffee, I even started thinking *"how it tests, feels, and the things I used to do when drinking"*

So again, I reminded myself that this is only for 7 days. Till around 8:00 AM everyone from my family was awake, so I went outside, had breakfast, and spent time with them.

After that, I had to do something else. I would have either drunk coffee, sugar, or something else and my Dopamine Detox would have ended right there.

But I didn't do such things. Instead, I set up the lights, cameras, and laptop.

And, I started shooting videos for YouTube, I did this till evening. Shot two videos, edited the same, and kept them on my computer. Normally, I don't shoot two videos in a single day, sometimes, I don't even shoot one.

But, this was different, I had plenty of time to kill and I used that time to do some work. At around 6:00 PM, I had dinner with my family and went to sleep at 8:00 PM.

This too was different as I normally go to sleep at 9 to 9:30 PM. The dinner was on time, no changes there.

Day 1 ended at 8:00 PM.

(Social Media wasn't really hard because I had cracked that years ago. For those who have a hard time quitting social, I will cover this in the movement)

Day 2

Day 2 was kind of easy compared to Day 1 because I had figured out what went wrong on day 1.

So I woke up at 5:00 AM, did all the normal things, and this time, I went outside at 5:30 AM for a walk.

This was a game-changing movement.

For about 30 minutes, I was outside of my house. No one was there, except for a few dogs.

When I reached my home, I exercised for about 30 minutes, took a bath, and had breakfast with my family.

At around 9:25 AM, I wrote a newsletter and scheduled the same for the evening. By the way, you can join BookiesTalk Newsletter. It's free.

Now, this too was different because I don't write a Newsletter on Friday. The newsletter schedule is every Sunday at 9:00 AM (IST).

After that, I wrote a new article for BookiesTalk and made some changes to other articles.

Around 11:30 AM, I had lunch, and after 1 hour, I shot intro footage for the Dopamine Detox Video. I also edited the same and kept all the footage.

After the launch, I wrote another article on Bookiestalk along with a few new web stories.

Again, the same, I had dinner at 6:00 PM and went to sleep at 8:00 PM.

Day 3

Day 3 was easy because I went to a new city with my family. We also went to one of our relatives and spent all day there. So day 3 ended.

I was busy all day long and I was with my family, so everything felt good while I didn't even think about Dopamine detox or even coffee.

Yes, I had to say No to Coffee and Tea with a heavy heart to relatives.

Day 4, 5, 6 and 7

I won't repeat the same things, like, I woke up at 5:00 AM and things I did because you already know that.

On day 4, I knew that I was doing Dopamine detox. So I just accepted that and went ahead with the day.

Did all the things, like, Shooting videos, writing articles, editing a few videos, reading books, exercising, and going out with Friends.

What I learned on days 4,5, 6, and 7 was,

The first two days are very hard (The last day will be easiest), I mean very very hard but if you can pass the first two days then, it gets easy and you start accepting that, this is what it is now.

Your brain gets aware of the things you have been doing. It will for sure, force you to do something out of the box but if you can resist then everything will be fine.

So what you have to do is, just take care of day 1 and day 2 and the rest will be easy peasy.

Day 8

Finally, I enjoyed a cup of coffee while filming, and I've included it in the final cut.

I had it around 10 AM, which is the perfect time because the caffeine won't disrupt your sleep later when you go to bed at night.

Yes, day 8 went faster than day 1.

I didn't even realize that I was doing Dopamine Detox because I was enjoying my work. The first couple of days were a bit tough, but after that, everything started to feel much easier.

The question you might have is, will I quit coffee? the answer is NO, why would I.

Because I'm not someone who drinks two to three cups of coffee every day, I enjoy Coffee but only one cup in the morning.

Like I have said, you don't have to isolate yourself from the internet, use it if your work requires it. The idea of Dopamine Detox is to cut down on unnecessary things.

What to Do after Dopamine Detox

If you have followed every step then after 7 days, you will know where to spend your time but keep in mind, your mind is complex and it has all the memories.

So make sure you're aware of it and don't start using social media too often, movies, Porn, or anything else.

Keep it simple, use social media but for a few minutes, not for hours.

Remember, you started Dopamine Detox because you wanted to make a change in your life.

Now that you've achieved that change, stick to it. Going back to old habits will make it much harder to start over again.

I would suggest you write down your thoughts when you try Dopamine Detox for the first time, especially, write the first two days.

If you don't know how to write your thoughts, please visit "Writing A Thoughts" (chapter. 7).

It will be a big help. So whenever you feel like using social media, just go back and read the first two days. This will remind you of what happens when you use social media for hours.

Reminder, don't forget to write down your thoughts when you try dopamine detox for the first time. It doesn't matter where you write, just write your feelings.

In the same way, start adding a few extra things in your daily routines. Like reading books, doing meditation, exercising, going out for walks, or just running.

Deal with Social Media Addiction

I promised you, I'll talk about social media, so here we go.

When you try Dopamine Detox, you're not quitting Social Media for a lifetime, you're just quitting for a few days and after that, you can always use all these websites that you love using.

So keep this in mind when you try doing Dopamine Detox because this is a very important trick to fool your brain.

But if you tell yourself that I will quit social media for a lifetime then you won't be able to quit it. After a few days or even hours, you will come back on social media.

When you say, I will only do this for 7 or even 2 days. Your mind will be like only 2 days, this is not that hard, so do it, I'm with you.

If you play with your mind smartly then you can do whatever you want. You just need to understand how your brain works.

Remember, the brain doesn't like drastic changes but if the changes are small and for a few days, it doesn't give you a hard time.

Even after doing all this, you will have the urge to use social media but you just have to keep it inside and don't use it because this is the key movement of your life.

If you manage to keep your distance from social media for the first 24 hours then the next day will be very easy because you have completed day 1 without social media.

The key part here is to complete the first 24 hours and you will be more than okay on the next day. Your brain treats this like a reward. So from the next day, it won't force you as much as it did on day 1.

So be aware of your actions and see where you're spending your time. Do whatever you want to do, just don't start using your smartphone and social media for 5 to 6 hours.

You're not doing this for me or anyone else, this is for you and only you. Whatever benefits you will get are for you. So take care of yourself because that's your job.

Risk of Dopamine Detox

Dopamine Detox is not scientifically proven and some scientists even believe that quitting social media, movies, TV shows, stopping masturbation, or even Sex can lead to,

- Anxiety
- Depression
- Fatigue
- Irritability
- Difficulty concentrating
- Sleep problems
-

The reason for these problems is that quitting everything can leave you feeling empty, making it hard to focus on other things.

My advice would be, don't try to quit everything. Try to quit a few things. Like Social Media, Coffee, masturbation, Porn, Movies, or something else.

Remember to Stay active, do what you love, and stay close to loved ones. Balance makes change easier.

Also, Dopamine Detox will be different for different people. You might not feel anything new after seven days while other people can feel like they are in heaven.

Final Edits

The idea of Dopamine Detox is not to unplug yourself from social media, masturbation, porn, sex, gaming, movies, or even materialistic things.

The idea is to have control over Dopamine and use this neurotransmitter to your advantage rather than being addicted to it.

- Be aware of your actions and see,
- How many hours do you spend on a smartphone
- How many cups of coffee do you drink every day
- How many porn videos do you watch every day
- How many times do you masturbate
- Why you don't feel like exercising
- Why do you love reading threads on X /(Twitter) rather than reading books?

Dopamine Detox won't change your life drastically but it can give you the right path that you can follow. In the end, you have to take action and keep in mind, you have a choice.

Chapter 9

Depth of Burnout

"Burnout is what happens when you try to avoid being human for too long." – Michael Gungor

Remember **"Burnout occurs when the lines between who you are and what you do become blurred."**

In simple words, Burnout happens when work and stress take over your life.

It can be caused by too much work, not knowing what's expected, no support, ignoring self-care, trying to be perfect, or working on things that don't add any value.

As Jeff Bezos says
"I think stress comes from not being clear about what you're trying to do. If you're trying to do everything, you're going to be overwhelmed. If you're clear on what you're trying to do, stress is much easier to handle."

This simply means it's not about the number of tasks you have, but your ability to prioritize and focus on what truly matters.

Doing work for 5 or even 8 hours a day doesn't cause burnout or stress but if you're working on something that doesn't matter at all then after some time, you will feel like *"What the heck I'm doing with my life, the same thing, wake up, do work, and go to sleep"*

Rather focus on high-priority tasks that align with your vision, and let go of smaller distractions.

By having a clear sense of purpose and control over decisions, it's easier to manage stress.

For example, I have lots of things to do in a day,

- Writing article for BookiesTalk.com,
- Making YouTube videos,
- Uploading them to social media,
- Writing this book, and
- Working on a few smaller ebooks.

Now, if I do everything every day then yes, I will be filled with stress and the day will come and I won't feel like working at all.

I chose to prioritize writing this book first thing in the morning. Everything else could wait until I finished a chapter or section.

Remember, focusing on important tasks and working on them will never give you stress but if you work on non-important tasks then there is a chance that the stress will build up day by day.

Things like using a phone for 4 hours, watching movies, playing games, or working on a project that doesn't require your attention will make your stress and anxiety go through the roof.

The end story is: focus on what matters most during the day. Otherwise, you'll end up doing nothing and spend the night overthinking it all. While choosing the task, use the **"Regret Minimization Framework.**

"The Framework says, Instead of focusing on what seems like the easiest or safest option right now, you think about the future and ask yourself: If I look back on this decision 10 or 20 years from now, will I be happy I made this choice?"

Once you answer this question, you will be free from everything because now you have a clear idea about where you need to focus.

Imagine you're thinking about starting your own business, but it feels risky.

So ask yourself, ***"If I don't do this now, will I regret not trying it in 10 years?"*** If your answer is yes, you're minimizing future regret, even though it might be tough at the beginning.

Take Jeff Bezos as an example. Before starting Amazon, Jeff Bezos was working in a stable job in New York.

But he knew that if he didn't try starting his own company, he might regret it later in life.

He used the Regret Minimization Framework to decide to leave his job and move to Seattle to start Amazon. He focused on what he'd regret less in the future—not starting the company—and took the risk.

Face It

When you have a problem in your life, face it, don't ignore it otherwise. It will build up like a pressure cooker and the day will come– it will explode.

Think for a second,
What will happen if you face fear, problems, or anxiety?
Will it kill you?
The answer is no.
The thing is we fear uncertainty.

When we don't know what's coming next, we worry about how it might affect our life, our family, or the way we live. Because of this fear, we tend to avoid facing the problems.

"Fear is only as deep as the mind allows."

This means that fear often comes from our own minds. Once we confront it, it becomes easier to manage.

Final Edits

- Remember, stress doesn't come from having too much to do, but from not deciding what to focus on.
- Set a limit on how much you work each day, week, or month. Don't overdo it—focus on what really matters.
- It's better to focus on one task and do it well, instead of trying to do many things at once.
- You don't have to be perfect. If you make mistakes, learn from them and move on, instead of getting stuck on them.
- If you feel like you're working too much, step back and take a look at what you've been doing. Decide what's most important and focus on that.
- When you feel like burnout, stop working, spend time with your loved ones, focus on your health, and do what you really want to do rather than ignoring the problems.
- Don't be busy all the time doing work that doesn't matter.

Chapter 10

Human Body

Exercise, a healthy body, and a balanced lifestyle work together like a well-tuned engine; when you care for each part, you create a life full of energy, resilience, and well-being.

Let me start this chapter with a quote from Eddie Jaku;

"I am still in awe of the human body and what it is capable of.

I am a precision engineer, and I have spent years making the most complicated, intricate machinery, but I could not make a machine like the human body.

It is the best machine ever made.

It turns fuel into life, can repair itself, and can do anything you need it to.

That is why today it breaks my heart to see the way some people treat their bodies, ruining this wonderful machine we are all gifted by smoking cigarettes, drinking alcohol, and poison.

They are demolishing the best machine ever put onto this Earth, and it is such a terrible waste"

In December 2022, I read The Happiest Man on Earth and found myself asking: How can the human body endure so much and still survive?

The kind of torture Eddie Jaku suffered during his time in the Holocaust is unimaginable.

And the funny thing is, these days people are suffering from diabetes, back pain, are overweight, have heart attacks, and still, consume more packaged foods.

As of now (2024), India has the second-largest population of people with diabetes, around 77 million, while China leads with approximately 140.9 million.

The worst part? Most people are aware of what causes diabetes —yet they ignore the basics. It's not rocket science:

- Avoid packaged foods.
- Limit carbohydrate intake.
- Cut down on processed sugar.
- And most importantly, prioritize regular exercise and a balanced, healthy diet.

What needs to change isn't just behavior, but mindset. Just because something isn't causing immediate harm doesn't mean it won't lead to serious consequences down the road.

It's similar with exercise. We know that working out for 30 days won't give us big muscles, so many people quit because they don't see instant results.

If you don't like to exercise then do some sort of physical movement during the day. Maybe play some sort of sports, go out for walks, go out running, or do yoga.

You won't live forever, but while you're here, a healthy body is one of the best assets you can have. Later in life, you may regret not prioritizing exercise and healthy eating, so why wait?

Don't treat your body like a trash can. Sure, enjoy the occasional indulgence, but don't let it become a habit. Invest in your health today, and it will repay you for a lifetime.

If possible, seek out someone who has struggled with and overcome addiction. They can share valuable insights on the mistakes they made and the lessons they've learned, offering guidance on what to avoid.

However, finding and approaching such a person may not be easy, and discussing these topics can be sensitive.

Instead, I recommend reading **Friends, Lovers, and the Big Terrible Thing by Matthew Perry.**

In the book, he talks about how he deals with addiction and much more.

He (Matthew Perry) says,

"The hardest part isn't starting recovery—it's sticking with it every day, even when it feels impossible."

Because of Friends (TV show), I learned to speak and write English and it was heartbreaking to read the story of Matthew Perry. This book will make sure that you never become addicted to anything.

In the end, I want to leave you with

"Happiness does not fall from the sky; it is in your hands. Happiness comes from inside yourself and from the people you love. And if you are healthy and happy, you are a millionaire. – Eddie Jaku

Final Edits

- The human body is a temple, treat it with the respect it deserves.
- Don't fill your stomach with anything and everything you come across.
- You won't live forever, so take care of your body now, and it will take care of you when you get older.
- Spend time with older people—they'll give you a fresh perspective on life.

Chapter 11

Feeling Busy All the time?

"Digital minimalism is about using technology with intention, choosing quality over quantity in how we connect and engage." - Cal Newport

Johann Hari once said

"We have created a world where digital distractions continuously steal our attention, and as a result, we've lost the ability to focus on what matters."

A question for you, Have you ever felt busy even when you didn't do any work?

For example, let's say you started working on a project that needs to be finished within a week.

You worked for a few minutes, but then you got tired, so you decided to grab a coffee. The problem was, you brought your phone with you.

While making your coffee, you started scrolling through social media, and before you knew it, 30 minutes had passed.

You completely lost interest in the project and thought, *"I'll just start again tomorrow."*

Next thing you know, you're still scrolling, watching movies and TV shows. When you finally go to bed, you tell yourself, *"I was so busy all day, how am I going to finish this project tomorrow?"*

Even though you didn't actually get any real work done, you felt like you were busy. If this sounds familiar, then maybe—just maybe—you need Digital Minimalism.

Or perhaps you don't. Let's figure it out together...

Get Your Life Back

- **Declutter Regularly:** Delete apps, files, and subscriptions you don't use.
- **Set Boundaries:** Limit screen time and make certain areas no-tech zones (e.g., bedroom or dining table).
- **Prioritize Intentional Use:** Use devices with a purpose, not for mindless scrolling.
- **Schedule Offline Time:** Take regular breaks from screens, like a digital detox day.
- **Disable Notifications:** Turn off non-essential alerts to reduce distractions.
- **Unsubscribe:** Avoid unnecessary emails, newsletters, or social media accounts.
- **Quality Over Quantity:** Focus on meaningful content, not endless feeds.
- **Embrace Analog Alternatives:** Use physical books, notebooks, or offline activities when possible.
- **Set Tech-Free Routines:** Start and end your day without screens.
- **Track Progress:** Regularly evaluate your habits and adjust as needed.

The point of Digital minimalism is not to quit social media, the idea is to limit the usage. So you can focus your time and energy on things that are important.

As Simon Sinek says "
We can only focus on a few things at a time. If we constantly check our phones, we're losing our capacity to concentrate on what's truly important."

1. The 30-Day Digital Declutter

- **What is it?** A 30-day break from all non-essential digital activities, apps, or platforms. Stop using apps like Instagram, Facebook, X/(Twitter), tiktok, or any other short video apps.

- **How it helps:** It gives you a chance to reset, reflect on your usage, and identify which apps were wasting your time.

- **Example:** If you decide to take a 30-day break from social media, during this period, you remove all social media apps from your phone and avoid using them, only keeping them for essential tasks like work or communication.

- **Remember:** It's okay if you install social media apps for some time. We are humans and we will make mistakes, just remember, you can also uninstall all the apps again and start 30-Day Digital Declutter again.

2. Embrace Boredom

- **What is it?** Allow yourself to experience boredom without reaching for your phone. Enjoy your free time, the same time that you were wasting on social media.
- This doesn't mean you have to sit alone for hours.
- This means, rather focus on the things that matter the most. It could be doing exercise, working on a project, or maybe enjoying your free time.

- **How it helps:** It trains your brain to enjoy every moment without digital distractions. This will be for sure hard at once but after a few days, your brain will start to accept the new change.

- **Example:** If you find yourself waiting for a bus or standing in line, resist the urge to check your phone. Instead, use that time to think, observe your surroundings, or simply relax.

3. Before You Adopt

- **What is it?** Before adopting a new app, device, or digital service, evaluate whether it aligns with your values and if it truly adds value to your life.

- **How it helps:** This helps you avoid adding unnecessary clutter.
- If one of your friends says, hey, did you hear about this app, it's amazing. This is where you say, keep it to yourself.

- **Example:** Before downloading a new social media app, ask yourself if it will contribute to your goals or just distract you.
- If it's not essential, skip it. Recently, Instagram launched Threads which is the same as X (twitter).
- So ask yourself, why did you need to install and if you find the right answer that aliens with your goals then go ahead but if not then don't waste your time on it.

In the end, no matter how much you read about Digital minimalism, try the formulas, apply everything but if you don't stay consistent then you will come back to where you started in the first place.

So sit down, and ask yourself a few questions about how you want to live your life.

Whether you're happy with this scrolling or you want to live a happy and peaceful life that you have control over.

Keep in mind, Digital minimalism is a choice to focus on what truly matters, rather than getting caught in the endless scrolling.

Use your smartphone, laptop, and even PS5 but put a limit on it. Don't be like that person who sits on the sofa scrolling or playing games.

Chapter 12

Wants and Needs

"Personal growth comes from knowing the difference between wants and needs. Focusing on what you truly need builds a stronger foundation for a fulfilling life, while endless wants only create distractions."

Most of the time, we have a clear understanding of what our needs and wants are.

However, we often find ourselves leaning towards our wants because they provide us with temporary happiness in the moment. So first, let's understand the basics.

- **Needs**: A basic, safe place to live. For most people, this might mean renting a small apartment or buying a modest home that fits their budget. The main goal is to have shelter and feel secure.
- **Wants**: A bigger or more luxurious home in a prime location. Maybe it has a beautiful view, a backyard pool, or is close to high-end shops. For some, this brings additional comfort and satisfaction, even if it comes with a larger financial commitment.

Imagine someone buying a large house with a pool and a big yard, even though they live alone and only use a small part of it. They're prioritizing comfort and perhaps the image of success.

Others might look at that and wonder if it's "necessary," but to the buyer, it feels rewarding.

Let me give you my example, I don't usually play games, but if I wanted to, I'd have to take time away from things That really matters.

That means either my work would suffer, or I'd lose time I could be spending time with my family. Even after knowing this fact, I went on buying Play Station 5.

Now the question is, do I regret spending Rs 49,999 ($592.49)? The answer is YES. The problem was, I knew that I would never sit on a chair for hours to play games.

The reason I feel I bought the PS5 was my childhood.

I always wanted to buy a PlayStation but back then we didn't have the money but the day I started earning and when I saw PS5 on Amazon, I couldn't help myself. This was me back in 2020.

That PlayStation changed every single thing about my life, from that day and now, I have never spent a single rupee where I didn't see the need to.

Now, remember, don't spend money if you don't have any. I bought the PS5 because I had the money.

It wasn't like, If I spend 50k ($592.49), my life will be screwed. Yes, I'm talking about taking a loan or debt from someone.

During these 4 years, I also understood that, don't question if someone is spending their money on the things that they didn't need.

The person earning Rs 10,000 ($118) a month can spend money on a smartphone worth Rs 20,000 ($236) and that is okay. It is their money.

For him, that smartphone means a lot. Maybe, he wanted to buy that phone for a long time, maybe, it was his dream or maybe, it was an impulsive purchase.

Every person makes financial decisions based on their unique experiences, values, and goals.

Who are we to question their decisions? What makes sense for one person financially might not for another because we each have a different relationship with money.

Some people spend more on experiences, while others prioritize saving or investing. This doesn't mean one approach is better; it's just a reflection of personal priorities.

Someone might buy a new car every few years, even though it depreciates in value. To them, having a reliable, stylish vehicle brings peace of mind and joy.

For someone else, driving an older car and saving or investing the difference makes more sense. Both choices are valid based on their individual values.

The point is that we all come from different places financially, emotionally, and culturally, which shapes how we use money. Instead of judging, understand that what's right for one person might not work for another.

Everyone's money story is unique, and so are their choices.

A quote from one of my favorite books, The Psychology of Money by Morgan Housel

"People do some crazy things with money. But no one is crazy. People from different generations, raised by different parents who earned different incomes and held different values, in different parts of the world born into different economies, will experience money in different ways."

1. The Needs vs. Wants Checklist

Writing down the purchase you're about to make will make you think about your decision. Whether that is need or want.

I love to read books and I never buy a single book, I always buy more than 10 books at once.

Now, I do this because I'm running a website (bookiestalk.com) and YouTube where I talk about books.

So for you, borrowing books from the library or buying one or two that focus on areas you're actively working on is a practical option.

But, Buying multiple books on various topics just to have them, even if you don't plan to read them, is nothing but your want.

Let's say, you're working on time management, a need would be purchasing a single, highly-rated book on the topic.

A want would be buying several productivity books at once without a plan to read or apply what you learn from each.

Sometimes, spending money on wants doesn't harm anyone but doing it over and over will make you broke.

2. The Rule of Opportunity Cost

- This approach involves evaluating each purchase by
  considering what else that money could go toward, helping
  people weigh the trade-off between needs and wants.

- **Example**: If buying a Rs 49,999 ($592.49) gadget, consider if
  that money could be better used on an emergency fund or a
  skill-building course. This comparison helps assess the true
  value of each purchase.

- This doesn't mean you shouldn't spend money on your
  wants, this only means, spend as much as you can afford
  too. If you're making Rs 20,000 ($236) and if you plan to
  buy an iPhone then it doesn't make any sense.

3. The 50/30/20 Rule (Elizabeth Warren & Amelia Warren Tyagi)

1. 50% for needs
2. 30% for wants
3. 20% for savings and debt repayment

- **How it helps:** By prioritizing needs and setting a specific allowance for wants, it helps avoid overspending on non-essentials and ensures that important bills and savings goals are covered.

- **Example:** If you earn $3,000 per month, $1,500 would go toward essentials like rent and groceries, $900 toward discretionary spending like dining out or hobbies, and $600 toward savings or paying off debt.

There you have it, now ask yourself what are your wants and needs. Whenever you plan to spend money, ask these kinds of questions and it will save you time and money as well.

By focusing on needs, you spend on things that actually contribute to your growth.

Maybe here and there you spend money on your wants, but don't make it a habit like buying a new iPhone every year or buying books that you will never read.

Chapter 13

What People Say...

"Your worth isn't defined by outside voices; it's built from within. Trust your own path and let your inner compass guide you."

"Your worth isn't defined by outside voices; it's built from within. Trust your own path and let your inner compass guide you."

I used to be the person who cared too much about other people's opinions.

We've all been there — wondering, 'If I try this and it fails, what will I say to all those people who told me it wouldn't work?'

The funny part is, First, you'll hear it from your family: *"I told you it wouldn't work. Look at my hair—it didn't turn white from sunshine! Just get a regular job, like we did. Taking risks isn't for us—we're not that rich."*

At first, a little criticism can be motivating—it pushes us to keep working toward our dreams. But after a certain point, it crosses into negativity, and that's not okay.

You can't just go to every single person and say, don't say this or that. What you do with your life is up to you. Don't let other people's opinions distract you.

As David Icke says, **"The greatest prison people live in is the fear of what other people think."**

Focus on what's important, and things will work out. But if you let others control how you act, you might fail—and end up blaming them instead of taking responsibility.

Imagine you're spending your time worrying about what people think of you, stressing over every little mistake, or trying to please others.

Now, picture yourself reflecting on the fact that life is short. Would you want to spend your time on stressing over every little mistake?

As Paul Kalanithi puts it **"The fact of death is unsettling. Yet there is no other way to live."**

This means that while thinking about death can be scary, it's also a reminder that life is short.

By keeping death in mind, he started to let go of things that didn't matter, like small worries or distractions. He chose to focus on what truly brought him joy.

He also writes, **"Even when the cancer has spread, I will continue to live the life I have chosen."**

This helped him focus on spending time with his family and continuing his work as a doctor, doing what gave him purpose, even in his last days.

Paul Kalanithi is the author of When Breath Becomes Air, one of my all-time favorite books.

Easiest Way to Say No

I used to find it hard to say No to anyone, especially to those who were family.

I was spending more time doing other people's work than focusing on my goals. One of the worst things humans do to each other is Emotional blackmail is

As Stephen Covey Says **"You have to decide what your highest priorities are and have the courage—pleasantly, smilingly, unapologetically—to say no to other things."**

Imagine You have a friend who always asks you to help them move or do favors, even when you're busy or don't feel like it.

You want to be helpful, but you're constantly exhausted and don't have the time or energy. If you keep saying "yes," you'll burn out, and eventually, start feeling bitter.

To set a boundary, you can politely but firmly say, "I'm sorry, I can't help you this time. I've got a lot on my plate right now."

Let me put it this way: saying no will never be easy, no matter who you say it to or where. Even if you ask for time and promise to help later, people will still get upset.

Just say no whenever you feel like you don't have enough time.
This has worked for me and I'm sure it will work for you.

You will for sure upset a few people but that will give you time
and energy to work on your dream.

Final Edits

- Don't waste too much time focusing on what others say. Focus on what truly matters and dedicate your energy to that, instead of worrying about other people's opinions.

- Learn to say no when necessary.

- Prioritize the people who truly matter to you—your family, such as your mother, father, siblings, spouse, or children. They are the ones who deserve your care and attention.

- People can be self-centered; they often don't really care about others. Keep this in mind, and you'll start to understand how people act when they want something from you.

- You don't have to go to every event or party just to make others happy. Go only when you really want to and have the time. Don't put your own priorities aside for events you don't care about.

As Anne Lamott says
"No is a complete sentence" - Remember this till you die"

Chapter 14

How to Talk To Anyone

"The best conversations happen when you stop worrying about being perfect and just focus on being yourself."

I know, it's a bit hard to talk to anyone, especially, if you're introverted but we're living in different times, so the day will come and you will have to.

Maybe that day won't come tomorrow but it will for sure come. Whether you're planning to do a job or even business. Even if you have enough money to live, you will need a skill to talk to anyone.

If talking to someone makes you nervous, remember, it's normal to feel that way. The key to getting better at conversations is to start small and practice regularly.

(Pro tip: Use ChatGPT or any other AI chatbot to practice starting conversations. If you're a guy, choose a female voice for an added challenge. This can help ease you into real-world interactions by building your confidence in a low-pressure environment.)

Focus on listening, ask simple questions, and try not to overthink. The more you engage with others, the easier it will become.

Look, from my personal experience, I feel that listening is the key because you will get to know about the person you're talking to.

For better understanding, let me tell you a story.

This time, Raj knows too much about how to talk with people, so instant, we will call his close friend, Ravi.

Ravi had always struggled with talking to people. It wasn't that he didn't want to connect with others, but he just didn't know how.

He would get nervous, his words would get stuck, and he would always worry about saying something wrong.

The worst part was when he had to talk to girls. He felt like no matter what he said, it would always come out awkward.

He would think, *"What if they don't like me?"* or *"What if I say something stupid?"*

This fear made him avoid conversations as much as possible.

One day, he saw Raj talking to girls. He went over to him and asked, "How are you doing this? I remember you used to get nervous talking to anyone."

Raj smiled and said, "Yeah, I used to be nervous, but then I realized I only have one life. Who cares what people think? I just want to live my life the way I want."

He also mentioned all the things he had learned, like habits, dopamine detox, the power of movement, and how he manages his thoughts.

After a few days, Ravi realized that if he wanted to improve, he couldn't keep avoiding people.

He had to face his fear. So, he decided to start small and take it one step at a time. He knew that he couldn't suddenly be great at talking to people, but he could get better with practice.

He began by having small chats with his friends. It didn't have to be anything deep—just simple conversations.

He might ask them about their day or talk about something they both enjoyed. At first, it was still hard, and Ravi felt the nerves creeping in. But the more he practiced, the easier it became.

He began to realize that most conversations didn't need to be perfect. People weren't judging him as harshly as he thought. They were just interested in talking, too.

The more Ravi practiced, the more he learned to focus on the other person.

He realized that asking someone about their day or their opinions made the conversation flow naturally.

It was less about what he said and more about being genuinely interested in the other person. Instead of worrying about what he should say next, he just listened.

And when he listened, the words came easier.

Ravi also realized something important: he didn't need to be perfect. It was okay to mess up sometimes.

If he said something that didn't make sense, he learned not to stress about it. Everyone made mistakes, and it was okay to laugh at yourself.

The more relaxed he became, the more others were relaxed too. It was okay to be imperfect.

When Ravi had to talk to girls, he remembered the same things he had learned. He stopped overthinking and just treated them like anyone else.

He asked questions, listened to their responses, and shared his own thoughts. Instead of worrying about what they would think of him, he just focused on the conversation.

The more he practiced, the easier it became to talk to anyone, even girls.

One of Ravi's biggest breakthroughs came when he realized that he didn't have to try to sound smart or impress anyone. He just had to be himself.

Once he stopped pretending to be someone else, he found that conversations felt much more natural.

Ravi's confidence grew as he practiced, and soon, talking to people didn't feel so scary anymore.

It wasn't about having perfect conversations or saying the right thing all the time—it was about connecting with others, being curious, and learning from each conversation.

Over time, Ravi learned to enjoy talking to people, whether they were strangers or close friends, and even with girls. The more he practiced, the easier it got.

I know it feels hard to do what Ravi did but it's not impossible.

Remember this: if you get nervous while talking to someone, it's completely okay.

Instead of worrying about how you come across, just focus on being yourself and having a genuine conversation.

People are usually more focused on their own thoughts and feelings than on judging you.

So, let go of any pressure or fear of making mistakes

Chapter 15

Fear of Stage

"The fear of speaking in public is just a reminder that you are about to do something meaningful. Embrace it, and the rest will follow."

Ravi felt more comfortable talking to people in everyday situations, he realized something important: if he could have casual conversations, maybe he could take it a step further and speak in front of a group.

The thought of public speaking, however, terrified him. Just the idea of standing in front of a crowd made his heart race.

He imagined himself stumbling over his words, and the thought of people judging him made him want to hide.

He knew it wasn't going to be easy, but he also knew that it was possible if he took small steps, just like he did with everyday conversations.

He started by speaking in front of smaller groups. At first, it was just his close friends.

Slowly, he became more comfortable with the idea of speaking in front of others, even if it was just a small crowd. He didn't worry about saying everything perfectly.

Ravi's next step was to join a local group where people practiced public speaking.

At first, it felt like a big leap, but once again, he reminded himself that it wasn't about perfection. It was about trying, learning, and improving over time.

He started giving short talks in front of the group. He would still feel nervous, but the more he did it, the easier it became.

The group offered him constructive feedback, and he used it to get better each time.

He also learned to reframe his fear. Instead of thinking, **"What if I mess up?"** he started thinking, **"I'm excited to share something valuable with the audience."**

The fear never fully went away, but Ravi realized that the nerves were just a part of the process.

*("Okay, I get it, not everyone is like Ravi. You might find it difficult to even have a simple conversation with someone. But here's the thing—remember, you only have one life." So f*ck that fear and have conversation or go on stage and say something. who gives a shit about what people say.)*

Sometimes, the hardest step is just starting. It may seem scary to step out of your comfort zone, but doing things alone can actually help you grow.

Try going out by yourself—eat alone, take a walk by yourself, or even go to the theater alone. At first, it might feel awkward or lonely, but after a few weeks, you'll start to see things differently.

You'll realize that being alone doesn't have to be a bad thing. In fact, you might even start enjoying your own company. The most important thing to remember is not to get caught up in worrying about what others might think.

Stop asking yourself, *"What if they judge me?"* or *"What if I make a mistake?"*

It's easy to get stuck in that cycle of overthinking, but it only holds you back. The truth is, most people are too focused on themselves to really care about what you're doing.

Forget the "what ifs."

Stop imagining all the possible scenarios that might go wrong. Instead, just take action.

Do what you feel like doing, without stressing about the future or the outcome.

The more you do this, the more you'll learn to trust yourself and the less you'll worry about what others think.

You'll realize that life is much easier when you stop waiting for the perfect moment or the perfect words. Just live in the moment and enjoy the experience.

Chapter 16

I'm Dad Now

When I found out I was going to be a dad, I made one thing clear to my family even before my son, Aarav, was born.

I said, *"No one will give him packaged foods, sugar, tea, coffee, smartphones, or outside food."*

I had seen kids who couldn't even eat a meal without a smartphone in hand, who refused to eat home-cooked food and only wanted packaged snacks.

That was something I didn't want for my son. Despite my best efforts to set these boundaries, relatives are relatives.

They'd occasionally give him packaged food when I wasn't around.

And when I asked, *"Why did you do that?"* The response I often got was, *"Your kid isn't any different. We've raised kids, and nothing happened to them. We know what we're doing."*

It was frustrating. Not that they didn't know how to raise kids, but because I didn't want Aarav to become dependent on things he didn't fully understand or need.

Now, you might be wondering: what's the big deal? What could possibly happen if my child eats outside food or uses a smartphone?

So, let's begin the class.

There was a girl named Lily who grew up surrounded by packaged snacks, sugary drinks, and a tablet for entertainment.

Whenever Lily wants a treat or something to do, she knew she could grab chips or ask for a soda, and her parents would give it to her.

She spent hours playing on her tablet every day, and this became her routine.

As Lily got older, she started to feel tired often and found it hard to focus in school. When she sat down to do homework, her mind would wander, and she would crave something sweet.

If she didn't have her tablet or her favorite snacks, she felt restless and would easily get annoyed.

Because she'd grown used to instant satisfaction, she struggled to find joy in slower activities, like reading or playing outside.

Eventually, Lily started feeling anxious and moody, but she couldn't quite understand why. Her parents began to worry about her low energy, but by then, the habits had already settled in.

Her thoughts often revolved around wanting her tablet, getting more sweets, or feeling bored quickly.

This can also lead to other addictive stuff that the kids can consume without telling their parents.

Remember, "Using something too much makes it less effective, so we need more to feel the same." For example, if a kid eats their favorite candy every day, it might stop being as exciting, and they'll need to eat more to feel the same joy.

When a child grows up with easy access to sugary snacks, packaged food, and screens, they may struggle with things like focus, energy levels, and self-regulation.

Also, kids are kids and they don't understand words like habits or how to break the loop.

They just want to feel good, if that feeling is coming from packaged foods, sugar, tea, coffee, smartphones, or outside food then it's not a good sign.

Remember, your kids didn't choose to come on this earth. You made that choice for them.

Now, it's your responsibility to give them a better life. Better life doesn't mean giving them whatever they want.

A better life starts from a healthy lifestyle.

As Janet
Lansbury says

"What we teach kids to value will shape how they handle the world as adults."

In the end, it's all about balance. Giving kids a taste of everything, but also showing them that joy doesn't always come from a quick treat or a screen.

It can be in spending time together, playing, or just taking it slow. These small things can make a huge difference as they grow.

Spend as much time as you can with your kids, they need you and they want to play with you.

Remember, the childhood of your kids will never come back.

So enjoy whatever time is left till they start to walk or talk.

In the end, when your kids grow up, they won't share everything with you, even the problems they're having.

So make them comfortable with you.

Don't raise your hands, shout at them, or force them to do something that they don't want to do.

As I'm writing this, my son has just opened the door to my room and is crawling towards me.

He can't speak yet, but he makes little noises whenever he wants something or is trying to show me something.

It's hard to write when he is around but still, it feels good when he is around.

I never imagined I could love another human being this much, but here I am.

Chapter 17

Master Your Sleep

"Sleep is the golden chain that ties health and our bodies together." – Thomas Dekker

Before we dive into this chapter, I want to warn you—it might feel a bit boring, as we're going to talk about sleep. There will be some new terms and concepts along the way.

If you're not in the mood to read right now, no worries—just set the book aside. When you're ready, come back. You will find me here.

The Importance of Sleep

We all know we need sleep, but few understand why. Sleep is not just a time for our bodies to rest; it's a period where essential processes occur.

From physical repair to mental rejuvenation.

During sleep, the body heals itself. It repairs muscles, builds tissues, and strengthens the immune system. But sleep doesn't just affect the body—it has a massive influence on the brain too.

This is when your brain works to store memories, regulate emotions, and clear out the waste products that accumulate during the day. Without sleep, your brain and body simply cannot function at their best.

1. Circadian Rhythm

This is your internal clock. It runs on a 24-hour cycle, guiding when you should be awake and when you should be asleep.

Your body is naturally in sync with the rising and setting of the sun, making light the most important cue for your circadian rhythm.

In the morning, exposure to sunlight signals your body to wake up, while darkness in the evening signals it's time to wind down.

Now, the question you might have is.

I know there are people who sleep during the day and work at night. So what about those, will they face any sort of health issue in the long run?

If a person consistently sleeps during the day and stays awake at night for years, their body may adapt to some extent, but it's likely to still face health consequences.

The circadian rhythm remains influenced by light exposure, and disrupted sleep patterns can lead to chronic issues like sleep disorders, hormonal imbalances, increased risk of cardiovascular diseases, poor cognitive function, and mood disturbances.

While the body might try to adjust, the long-term effects are still damaging, especially to mental and physical health. The damages that person will face are.

- **Impaired Cognitive Function:** Poor sleep affects memory, focus, and decision-making.
- **Weakened Immune System:** Less sleep increases vulnerability to illness.
- **Increased Risk of Chronic Conditions:** Higher chances of obesity, heart disease, diabetes, and stroke.
- **Mental Health Issues:** Increased risk of anxiety, depression, and mood disorders.
- **Hormonal Imbalance:** Disrupted sleep can alter hunger and stress hormones.

2. Adenosine

This is a chemical in your brain that builds up the longer you stay awake.

As the day goes on, adenosine builds up in your brain, making you feel increasingly tired and ready to sleep. This is your body's natural signal to rest.

When you consume caffeine, it blocks adenosine's receptors, preventing you from feeling tired and keeping you alert.

But when you sleep, your brain naturally clears away this accumulated adenosine, allowing you to wake up feeling refreshed and restored.

Now, you might have questions like. What happens inside my brain when I take caffeine just before bedtime.

When you drink caffeine close to bedtime, it interferes with your brain's natural ability to process adenosine.

Normally, adenosine builds up throughout the day, signaling to your brain that it's time to sleep.

Caffeine blocks adenosine's receptors, making it harder for you to feel tired.

This disrupts your sleep cycle, preventing you from reaching deeper stages of rest, and can lead to fragmented sleep.

As a result, your brain doesn't clear the accumulated adenosine, making you feel less refreshed when you wake up.

This is one of the reasons why you feel tired even after a full night's sleep. One of the reasons could be, you're drinking Coffee or tea just before a bad time.

What Happens When We Don't Sleep Enough?

Research indicates that people who sleep less than six hours a night are more likely to gain weight and develop type 2 diabetes due to disrupted hormones that regulate hunger and metabolism.

A lack of sleep also causes an increase in stress hormones like cortisol, which leads to further health complications. Furthermore, chronic sleep deprivation has a significant impact on mental health.

People who consistently get too little sleep are at a greater risk of developing mood disorders like depression and anxiety.

Studies have shown that even a few days of insufficient sleep can lead to irritability, stress, and negative mood swings, and these symptoms tend to improve once sleep patterns are restored.

Not getting enough sleep doesn't just make you tired—it can harm your health. Lack of sleep affects how well you remember, focus, and make decisions.

It also weakens your immune system, making you more likely to get sick. Over time, it increases the risk of serious conditions like heart disease, stroke, and diabetes.

The Stages of Sleep

Sleep isn't just one thing—it's a series of stages, each with its own important role. A typical sleep cycle lasts about 90 minutes, and it repeats several times throughout the night. There are two main categories of sleep: non-REM sleep and REM sleep.

1. Non-REM Sleep: This is the restorative phase of sleep. It has three stages:

- **Stage 1 (Light Sleep):** This stage marks the transition from wakefulness to sleep. Your muscles relax, and your brain waves slow down. You might experience a sensation of "falling," which can cause a sudden twitch or startle that briefly wakes you up. This stage is brief, typically lasting only a few minutes.

- **Stage 2 (Deeper Relaxation):** In this stage, your body temperature drops, heart rate slows, and breathing becomes steady. Your body continues to prepare for the deeper stages of sleep. You are less likely to be disturbed, and this stage occupies the majority of your sleep cycle.

- **Stage 3 (Deep Sleep):** Also known as slow-wave sleep, this is when your body undergoes restoration. It's the most rejuvenating phase, where tissue repair, immune system strengthening, and muscle recovery happen. Waking up from this stage can leave you feeling groggy and disoriented.

2. REM Sleep (Dreaming): During REM sleep, your brain becomes very active, and vivid dreams occur.

While your mind is engaged, your body is temporarily paralyzed to prevent you from acting out dreams.

REM sleep is vital for memory consolidation, emotional regulation, and cognitive functions such as learning and problem-solving.

Both non-REM and REM sleep are necessary for different reasons, and missing out on either one can disrupt your health and well-being.

How to Improve Your Sleep

Now that we understand the importance of sleep, how do we ensure we're getting enough of it? Here are some simple steps you can take to improve your sleep:

1. Stick to a Sleep Schedule:

Go to bed and wake up at the same time every day, even on weekends. This helps regulate your circadian rhythm and trains your body to fall asleep and wake up naturally.

2. Create a Relaxing Bedtime Routine:

Avoid screens, caffeine, and other stimulating activities in the hour or two before bed.

Instead, try reading, listening to calming music, or practicing relaxation techniques like deep breathing or meditation. This helps signal to your brain that it's time to wind down.

3. Make Your Bedroom Sleep-Friendly:

Your environment plays a big role in your ability to fall asleep. Keep your bedroom dark, quiet, and cool. If necessary, use blackout curtains to block out light or a white noise machine to drown out sounds.

A comfortable mattress and pillow can also make a huge difference in the quality of your sleep.

4. Limit Caffeine and Alcohol:

While caffeine might make you feel awake and alert during the day, it can interfere with your ability to fall asleep later.

Try to avoid caffeine at least 6 hours before bedtime. Alcohol might make you feel sleepy, but it disrupts the deeper stages of sleep, so it's best to limit your intake, especially in the evening.

5. Get Regular Exercise:

Physical activity can improve the quality of your sleep.

However, avoid intense exercise right before bed, as it can make it harder to fall asleep. Aim for moderate exercise during the day to help your body sleep better at night.

6. Get Exposure to Natural Light:

Your body's internal clock is heavily influenced by light. Try to get exposure to natural sunlight in the morning.

This helps reset your circadian rhythm and improves sleep quality at night. On the flip side, reduce exposure to bright lights in the evening to signal to your body that it's time to sleep.

6. Manage Stress:

Stress can make it difficult to sleep, as it keeps your mind racing at night.

Practicing relaxation techniques such as mindfulness, yoga, or journaling can help calm your mind and reduce stress.

If you're prone to overthinking at night, try writing down your thoughts before bed to clear your mind.

The Impact of Sleep on Mental Health

One study conducted by the American Psychological Association found that individuals who reported chronic sleep deprivation had a much higher incidence of anxiety and depression.

When you don't sleep well, your brain struggles to process emotions and manage stress.

This can make you more prone to anxiety, depression, and irritability. On the other hand, getting good sleep can improve your mood and make you more resilient in the face of stress.

REM sleep plays a crucial role in regulating emotions.

During this phase, your brain works to process emotional experiences from the day, organizing and storing memories related to feelings and experiences.

This process helps to make sense of and calm emotional responses.

The result is that after a full night of REM sleep, you often feel more balanced, centered, and better equipped to handle challenges.

This emotional stability is one of the reasons why a good night's sleep leaves you feeling refreshed and ready to face a new day.

The Importance of Sleep for Learning and Memory

During sleep, your brain consolidates new memories and strengthens the neural connections needed for learning.

This means that if you're trying to learn something new—whether it's studying for a test, picking up a new skill, or simply remembering important information—sleep plays a key role in making that learning stick.

When you sleep after learning something new, your brain doesn't just store the information—it actively strengthens and consolidates it, improving your ability to recall and apply it later.

A study involving a video game puzzle found that participants who napped after reaching an impasse were significantly more likely to solve the puzzle when they returned to it, compared to those who stayed awake.

Similarly, another study revealed that participants who slept after learning a challenging math puzzle were twice as likely to discover a hidden shortcut, a key to solving the puzzle more efficiently, than those who stayed awake.

These findings suggest that sleep is not just a passive activity; it actively helps the brain reprocess and reorganize information.

REM sleep, in particular, which is the stage of sleep where dreaming occurs, is essential for creative problem-solving.

In an experiment, participants who took a nap after working on a creative task were better at using newly acquired information to come up with innovative solutions.

In essence, sleep doesn't just help you retain what you've learned—it can make you better at thinking creatively, solving problems, and coming up with fresh ideas.

This is because sleep, particularly REM sleep, allows the brain to make new connections and reorganize thoughts, giving you a "mental reset" that enhances cognitive flexibility.

So, if you're working on a tough problem or trying to come up with new ideas, a good night's sleep might be your best strategy for success.

The Productivity Playbook

I love to explore productivity hacks, especially the ones with proper methods and rules. Over the years, I have collected a few of them, so let's take a closer look at them.

For you, I have categorized every section. So use this whenever you need it.

Also, there is no need to use every single method, it's just a waste of time. Pick any and start doing what matters the most.

For me, the Pomodoro Technique, Eisenhower Matrix, and 80/20 Rule work best. I've tried almost all of these methods, but these three are the ones I use every day to stay focused and get things done.

1. Pomodoro Technique

This is the best and most effective way to start and finish your work with 100% focus. The basic idea is to break your work into short, focused chunks with small breaks in between.

Each focused chunk is called a "Pomodoro," named after the Italian word for "tomato," inspired by a tomato-shaped kitchen timer that the creator, Francesco Cirillo, used to track time.

How it works

Pick a task you want to focus on (it could be reading, cleaning, or even a hobby).

1. Set a timer for 25 minutes – this is one Pomodoro.
2. Work on the task until the timer goes off. Try to ignore distractions and stay focused.
3. Take a 5-minute break when the timer rings. Stretch, grab a drink, or relax a little.
4. Repeat the cycle. After completing four Pomodoros, take a longer break, maybe 15–30 minutes.

2. Eisenhower Matrix (Urgent-Important Matrix)

This is what I use everywhere. I also talked about this in my first book "Productive Mindset" .

It's one of the best ways to decide what you should be focusing on.

This method was named after Dwight D. Eisenhower, a former U.S. president.

The matrix divides tasks into four quadrants: If you can make a box and make 4 lines, one in the vertical (middle) and one horizontal (again, middle).

- **Quadrant 1: Urgent and Important –** Tasks that need to be done immediately. For me it's writing this book, for you, it can be any of your work projects or something that needs to be done.
- **Quadrant 2: Not Urgent but Important –** Tasks that are valuable in the long run but don't need immediate attention. Exercise, you can skip in the morning and do the same before sunset.
- **Quadrant 3: Urgent but Not Important –** Tasks that demand attention now but aren't truly important to your goals. Maybe, buying groceries.
- **Quadrant 4: Not Urgent and Not Important –** Tasks that are neither urgent nor valuable; these are often distractions. Using a smartphone or watching movies.

Eisenhower once said, **"What's important is rarely urgent, and what's urgent is rarely important."**

3. D.I.S.S. Method

I searched everywhere but I didn't find who created this method, the answer I found was "It doesn't have a single creator" It combines ideas from various time-management and focus strategies.

By the way, I heard about this method from Tim Ferriss. D.I.S.S = Delete, Ignore, Separate, Simplify

How it works

- **Delete:** Get rid of distractions that aren't necessary. If something is taking up your time but isn't important, let it go.

- **Ignore:** For things that you can't remove but don't need to pay attention to right now, ignore them temporarily. This could mean putting your phone on silent or turning off notifications.

- **Separate:** If distractions are hard to ignore, separate yourself from them. Move to a different room, work in a quieter space, or use noise-canceling headphones.

- **Simplify:** If a task seems overwhelming, break it down into smaller, simpler steps. Tackling one small part at a time makes it easier to stay on track. Use the Pomodoro Technique.

As Tim Ferriss says **"Focus on being productive instead of busy." apply the same in your life from NOW.**

4. The 80/20 Rule

The 80/20 Rule, also known as the Pareto Principle. It suggests that 80% of results come from 20% of efforts.

This means that not all tasks are equally important—some things you do have a much bigger impact than others.

Let's see how you can find where you're putting your efforts.

How the 80/20 Rule works

- **Identify Key Tasks:** Look at everything you're working on and figure out which tasks are producing the most results. These are the tasks that fall in the 20% category.

- **Focus on High-Value Activities:** Once you know what the key tasks are, focus more of your energy on them. Spend less time on low-impact tasks.

- **Eliminate or Minimize the Rest:** Cut out or reduce time spent on tasks that only give small results (the 80%) so you can put more time into the important ones (the 20%).

- **Reassess and Improve:** Continuously check your tasks to see if the 80/20 distribution still holds true. As you make progress, the high-impact tasks might change, so keep refining your focus.

6. Kaizen (Continuous Improvement)

Kaizen is a Japanese concept that means **"continuous improvement."**

It's about making small, ongoing changes in daily routines to improve gradually over time. Rather than focusing on huge goals.

Kaizen encourages taking small steps every day to build momentum, improve skills, and make lasting changes. Kaizen can be applied in personal growth, work, health, and any area where you want to make steady progress.

Long story short, apply this technique wherever you like.

How Kaizen works

- **Identify Small Changes:** Start by identifying tiny adjustments you can make in your daily routine that would bring improvement over time. These changes should be simple and achievable. Don't make drastic changes that you find hard to even try.

- **Take Daily Steps:** Focus on doing these small actions every day. By staying consistent, the small steps add up and lead to meaningful progress over time.

- **Track Progress:** Keep track of the changes, no matter how small. Seeing progress builds motivation and reinforces the habit.

- **Reflect and Adjust:** Regularly review how these changes are helping you. If something isn't working, adjust it slightly to keep improving. The key is to keep moving forward without overwhelming yourself.

Kaizen and the 1% Rule are similar but Kaizen adds one layer on top. Kaizen originated in Japan after World War II while 1% Rule was popularized by James Clear in his 2018 book Atomic Habits.

7. Ikigai (Reason for Being)

The one you may have heard about. Ikigai is a Japanese concept that means "reason for being."

It's about finding purpose and meaning in life by balancing what you love, what you're good at, what the world needs, and what you can be rewarded for.

- **Identify What You Love:** Think about what activities or interests make you feel joyful and passionate. This could be a hobby, a subject you're drawn to, or anything that makes you feel alive.

- **Recognize What You're Good At:** Consider your strengths and skills—things you're naturally good at or have developed over time. Your ikigai often aligns with your unique talents.

- **Consider What the World Needs:** Reflect on how you can make a difference or contribute to others. Your ikigai should ideally have a positive impact, whether it's helping people, solving a problem, or creating something meaningful.

- **Find What You Can Be Rewarded For:** Think about how you can be compensated for this pursuit, either financially or in other fulfilling ways. This could mean a job, a side project, or a volunteer role that feels rewarding.

8. Wabi-Sabi (Embracing Imperfection)

Wabi-Sabi means **"embracing imperfection."** It's about finding beauty in things that are incomplete, flawed, or transient.

Instead of striving for perfection, Wabi-Sabi encourages acceptance of life's natural imperfections and appreciating things as they are.

How Wabi-Sabi works

- **Accept Imperfections:** Recognize that nothing is perfect, permanent, or complete. Embrace the natural imperfections in people, things, and situations, and find peace in that acceptance.

- **Find Beauty in the Incomplete:** Appreciate the beauty in things that are aged, weathered, or unconventional. Wabi-Sabi teaches us to see value in items or experiences that show signs of time and use.

- Practice Simplicity: Focus on simplicity and minimalism, valuing what's essential rather than aiming for lavish or idealized versions of things. This helps you appreciate what's real and meaningful.

- **Live Mindfully:** Wabi-Sabi is about being present and appreciating the current moment. By focusing on "what is" rather than "what could be," you learn to enjoy life as it unfolds.

You don't have to be perfect, you just need to be you. No one is perfect and it's okay to make mistakes. Just remember, you don't repeat those mistakes again.

"There is a crack in everything, that's how the light gets in." — Leonard Cohen

Now, if you want you can work for more than 25 minutes and take a 10-minute break. It depends on what kind of project you're working on.

Slowly, increase the Pomodoro from 25 to 60 minutes.

Imagine, you force yourself to work for 2 hours continually. Will this make you motivated to do it twice, the answer is NO.

An instant of doing work for 2 hours continually. Break your work into the pieces.

Do your work for 25 minutes, and take a 5-minute Break. Repeat the same for 4 times and you won't even notice that you have worked for 2 hours.

9. Shoshin "beginner's mind."

Shoshin encourages humility, letting go of assumptions, and staying open to new ideas. By adopting a beginner's mind, you keep a fresh perspective and remain receptive to growth and insight, no matter how familiar something seems.

- **Let Go of Preconceptions:** Approach situations without assuming you know everything. Shoshin teaches that even if you've done something many times, there's always something new to learn.

- **Stay Curious and Open**: Embrace a child-like curiosity and eagerness to explore. This openness helps you discover new insights and prevents you from becoming bored or complacent.

- **Accept Mistakes as Part of Learning:** Shoshin means valuing growth over perfection. Don't be afraid to make mistakes; see them as part of the learning journey.

- **Practice Humility:** Be humble, recognizing that you're always a student in some way. Humility helps you respect different perspectives and stay open to others' knowledge.

By letting go of "expert" expectations, you free yourself to explore and grow continuously. This mindset makes learning more fulfilling and lets you see life's experiences with fresh eyes, enhancing both growth and enjoyment.

"Every man I meet is my master in some point, and in that I learn of him." — Ralph Waldo Emerson

10. Shikata ga nai ("It Can't Be Helped")

Shikata ga nai is a Japanese phrase meaning "It can't be helped" or "There's nothing you can do about it." It reflects a mindset of accepting situations that are beyond your control.

Instead of resisting or worrying about things you can't change, Shikata ga nai encourages you to let go and focus on what you can control. This approach is deeply rooted in Japanese culture and is often used to cope with challenging situations calmly and practically.

"Grant me the serenity to accept the things I cannot change, courage to change the things I can, and wisdom to know the difference." – Reinhold Niebuhr

How Shikata ga nai works

Recognize when a situation is out of your control. Accept that there are some things you can't change, and resisting them only creates frustration.

- **Let Go of Frustration:** Instead of feeling stressed or upset, let go of the emotional weight that comes with trying to control the uncontrollable. This helps you stay calm and focused.

- **Focus on What You Can Do:** Redirect your energy toward things you can influence. Shikata ga nai doesn't mean giving up; it means letting go of the need to control everything and taking action where possible.

- **Move Forward:** Embrace the situation with a sense of acceptance. Moving forward with a calm mind allows you to handle challenges with resilience.

In the end, remember, there is no need to be overwhelmed by all the concepts. I added these just for your knowledge, remember it and apply whenever you need it.

Don't force yourself to apply each, if needed use them otherwise, pass it on to others.

Life's Last Edit

As you reach the end of Life's Last Edit, it's time to step back and look at the bigger picture.

Throughout this book, we've discussed many concepts—habits, purpose, movement, burnout, confidence, and so much more.

The first step to making meaningful changes in your life is recognizing that you have the power to take control.

Life doesn't just happen to you—it's shaped by the decisions you make every single day.

Whether you realize it or not, you're always editing your story. The key is learning how to edit it in a way that aligns with who you want to be.

Now, putting it all together means taking action. It's easy to get overwhelmed by the thought of transforming your entire life at once.

But that's not how change works. The small, consistent edits are what lead to the most powerful transformations.

Start small. Start today. Pick one thing—whether it's your morning routine, a healthier habit, or a shift in mindset—and commit to it. Over time, you'll see how each edit compounds to create lasting change.

Remember, this is not a destination—it's an ongoing process. Life will continue to throw challenges your way, and you will make mistakes.

But each time you edit your response, each time you make a small change to how you approach life, you're creating a better version of yourself.

The key is to stay committed to the process, trust the journey, and keep making those small edits until you're living a life that truly feels like yours.

1. Life's True Compass

Your life's direction begins with understanding your purpose and values. The compass you use to navigate life is built on clarity about what truly matters. Knowing where you want to go —what drives you—helps guide every decision you make, whether big or small.

2. Power of Movement

Staying in the present moment is where true growth happens. Movement, both physically and mentally, keeps you aligned with the now. Whether it's through exercise, mindfulness, or a simple change in perspective, movement helps you stay grounded and focused on what matters today.

3. 70,000 Thoughts

The constant stream of thoughts we have each day can either help or hinder our progress. Becoming aware of your thoughts and learning to control them is one of the most powerful tools you can use. Redirect your thinking, focus on positive actions, and stop allowing unhelpful thoughts to take charge.

4. Confident vs. Smart Person

Confidence is the real key to success, not just intelligence. Confidence comes from believing in your own abilities and taking action. Smartness may give you knowledge, but confidence empowers you to put that knowledge into action, even when faced with uncertainty.

5. Life's Little Seeds

Small actions often have the biggest impact. It's easy to overlook the little habits or decisions, but over time, they grow into something much larger. Just as a tiny seed grows into a big tree, small efforts compound into significant change.

6. For Better Tomorrow

The future is shaped by what you do today. Don't wait for tomorrow to take action; it's the small edits you make now that will create a better tomorrow. Keep your eyes focused on the future, but always take action in the present.

7. Writing Your Thoughts

Writing can be one of the most powerful tools for self-reflection and growth. By writing down your thoughts, you externalize them, giving you a chance to examine and edit them. It's like having a conversation with yourself, allowing you to see things from a new perspective.

8. Dopamine Detox

We live in a world where distractions are everywhere, and our brains are constantly craving stimulation. A dopamine detox can help reset your mind, giving you the clarity and focus needed to make the edits that will truly serve you.

9. Depth of Burnout

Burnout is real, and it can drain your energy and creativity. Recognizing the signs early on and knowing how to address them can prevent burnout from taking over. Take breaks, set boundaries, and prioritize your well-being—these are the essential edits to avoid burnout.

10. Human Body

The human body is designed for movement, health, and energy. Taking care of your body is essential for living a productive and fulfilling life. Exercise, proper nutrition, and adequate rest all play a crucial role in ensuring you have the energy to pursue your goals.

11. Feeling Busy All the Time?

Being busy doesn't always mean you're being productive. It's easy to get caught up in the hustle, but it's important to take a step back and assess whether you're spending your time wisely. Focus on what matters, eliminate distractions, and make space for what truly brings you value.

12. Wants and Needs

Understanding the difference between wants and needs is key to finding contentment and balance. Wants are fleeting desires, while needs are essential for your growth and well-being. By focusing on what you truly need, you can avoid falling into the trap of materialism and distractions.

13. What People Say

We often let the opinions of others guide our decisions. But remember, other people's thoughts are reflections of their own beliefs and experiences, not yours. Stay true to your path and edit your responses to criticism—don't let others dictate your story.

14. How to Talk to Anyone

Communication is essential for building connections and achieving your goals. The way you speak and listen can either create bridges or walls. Focus on listening, being present, and speaking with clarity. It's not about what you say, but how you make others feel when you speak.

15. Fear of Stage

Fear is natural, but it shouldn't hold you back. Whether it's public speaking or taking a big risk, facing your fears is how you grow. Every time you step outside of your comfort zone, you're editing your narrative, becoming a stronger and more confident version of yourself.

16. I'm Dad Now

Fatherhood brings a new level of responsibility and purpose. As a parent, you are constantly editing your story while guiding the next generation. Every lesson you teach your child is an edit to their story too. Your actions matter, and they create a legacy that lasts.

17. Master Your Sleep

Sleep is more than just rest; it's an essential part of your overall well-being. Quality sleep affects your mood, focus, and productivity. Edit your habits to ensure you're getting the rest you need to perform at your best.

"Life is not a final draft but an ongoing story— each day offers us a chance to edit, revise, and rewrite the life we want to live."

Author's Note

What I say about myself,

I love writing whether it's a book, article, newsletter, or even my thoughts. If you ever come across my book, at least take a look. You will find something interesting.

Next, I want to write a novel. I don't have a story in mind yet, but I'm excited to craft something truly story-driven.

Before that, two more short eBooks are on the way. They'll be quick reads, so be sure to check them out on shop.bookiestalk.com!

And that's a wrap. I hope you found value in this journey.

Remember, change doesn't happen overnight, but with consistent effort, you're already heading in the right direction. Keep moving forward, one step at a time.

Thank you for reading. I'm excited to see you grow, evolve, and live the life you truly deserve. Take care, stay focused, and make today count.

Until next time, this is Rahul Makwana, signing off.

What I say about myself,

I love writing whether it's a book, article, newsletter, or even my thoughts. If you ever come across my book, at least take a look. You will find something interesting.

Next, I want to write a novel. I don't have a story in mind yet, but I'm excited to craft something truly story-driven.

Before that, two more short eBooks are on the way. They'll be quick reads, so be sure to check them out on shop.bookiestalk.com!

And that's a wrap. I hope you found value in this journey.

Remember, change doesn't happen overnight, but with consistent effort, you're already heading in the right direction. Keep moving forward, one step at a time.

Thank you for reading. I'm excited to see you grow, evolve, and live the life you truly deserve. Take care, stay focused, and make today count.

Until next time, this is Rahul Makwana, signing off.